# WHEN

# WORLDS

# COLLIDE

Professors and presidents frequently write books. When one of our students writes one, particularly addressed to his peers, it's time to sit up and take notice! With biblical, honest, prophetic, and, yes, humorous insights into young adult culture, this book charts a path for younger adults to passionately live their faith. Rather than retreating into inactivity and lethargy, the Blackabys challenge their peers to pick up the banner of our faith and charge forward. When they do, worlds collide and the power of the gospel is experienced. Read this book and get ready to get moving!

—Jeff Iorg, president Golden Gate Seminary

Currently leaders debate the actual percentage of young people who drop out of church after leaving home. Regardless the actual number, it is entirely too high. Rather than calling youth and the church to "hold the fort" and hang in the church through the younger years, Mike and Daniel Blackaby challenge youth to do more: to aggressively "collide" with the culture for the sake of the gospel and the glory of God.

—Alvin L. Reid, PhD, professor of Evangelism and Student Ministry, Bailey Smith Chair of Evangelism, SEBTS

Mike and Daniel Blackaby carry the mantle of spiritual maturity and leadership for a new generation of believers. Their call to young Christians is of the highest order—to engage the culture—so that Christ might be glorified. To that end, the Blackaby brothers have written a "must read" book for believers who are not satisfied with the spiritual status quo.

—Todd Starnes, FOX News Channel

To find such a rich balance of wisdom and wit is rare; to find it in two young men in their twenties is even more so. Their self-effacing humor and boyish charm is winsome, but it's the solid writing and the firm grasp on following God through the touch stuff that makes this book a page turner for a far wider audience than twenty-somethings.

This message, packed with enough mirth to bring out the sun on your darkest day, crosses genders and generations because it packs a wallop of truth in the wrapping of merriment.

—Connie Cavanaugh, international speaker and author of
*Following God One Yes at a Time*

*When Worlds Collide* tackles one of the most needed discussions among young people today—How do we truly live our faith? As Christians, we seem to walk the precariously thin line of either carving into the world or hiding from it. Mike and Daniel use incredible humor and personal stories to lead their peers into a soul-searching journey that challenges them to collide with the world in ways that change it. In a generation that has fallen victim to lukewarm living, these brothers have raised the bar and set fire to the radical, authentic, and hardly boring way that Christ is calling us to live! These pages are ablaze and will inspire, strengthen, and renew.

—Paige Armstrong, speaker, writer, and recording
artist; CD titled *Wake Up*

# WHEN WORLDS COLLIDE

## MIKE AND DANIEL BLACKABY

B&H
PUBLISHING GROUP
Nashville, Tennessee

ISBN: 978-0-8054-6481-8


Published by B&H Publishing Group
Nashville, Tennessee


Dewey Decimal Classification: 248.83
Subject Heading: CHRISTIAN LIFE \ CHRISTIANITY
AND CULTURE

1 2 3 4 5 6 7 8 • 15 14 13 12 11

We dedicate this book with love and respect to our grandparents, Henry and Marilynn Blackaby, for colliding with the world long before we were ever born, and giving us a godly heritage for which we will always be grateful.

# ACKNOWLEDGMENTS

Special thanks to our mom and dad and our little sister Carrie for all the encouragement, editing, advice, and laughter throughout the process of writing this book.

Also, thanks to the following people who have invested in our lives in multitudinous ways over the years: Sarah (you've been a lifeline!), Craig and Marcy Hallden, Jonathan and Cathy Chisholm, the Brown family, Chad and Heather Hood, Jay and Joanna Mitchell, Lynn Dove, Kathy Seidler, Darin Ruff, Al and Karen Rayner, Ross and Phyllis Lincer, Pastor/Uncle Mel, Harold Harper, Gary Terashita (thanks for taking a chance on us!), Dr. Collier (for the encouragement and extra proofreading!), all the Cavanaugh and Blackaby aunts and uncles, JP (without whom this book would have far fewer anecdotes!), Chevy, and the many others who have walked with us and encouraged us along the way. You all rock!

# CONTENTS

# FOREWORD

In the middle of the nineteenth century, in a small church in Boston, Massachusetts, a Sunday school teacher named Edward Kimball had a burden to reach people for Jesus Christ. History does not record much about this man. In fact, most people have never heard of him, but he was a Collider, someone who simply shared the good news of Jesus Christ. This simple Sunday school teacher chose to collide with people to lead them to salvation in Christ. One day Edward Kimball decided to collide with one of his Sunday school students who worked as a shoe store clerk. As Kimball shared his hope in Jesus, the young man decided he wanted Jesus in his life. That day Kimball led Dwight Lyman Moody to the Lord. And what an impact Moody had around the world! He led many to Christ and started Moody Church and other Christian ministries. All of this because a Sunday school teacher decided to collide with one his students. But the story doesn't stop there.

As D. L. Moody grew in his walk with Christ, he felt the calling to be a preacher—to collide with the culture and the people of his day, especially in the Chicago area. Moody became one of America's all-time greatest preachers. He preached in revivals across America and in Europe. As he was preaching on one particular trip to England, Moody befriended another American evangelist named Wilbur Chapman. Chapman gave his life to Christ years before, but Moody encouraged him to keep preaching the gospel in order to see others come to know Christ. Chapman continued to preach around the world. Occasionally, Chapman would take along apprentices in order to mentor them. Just as Moody encouraged him, he too wanted to encourage others to impact the world. One of these apprentices was a man named Billy Sunday, a former professional baseball player.

Billy Sunday became a prominent revivalist in America. He led revivals around the country and had a profound impact on many people living in America in the early twentieth century. In 1924, Billy Sunday had such an influence in Charlotte, North Carolina, that the local Christian businessmen started the Billy Sunday Layman's Evangelistic Club. It was later renamed the Charlotte Businessmen's Club (CBMC). These men, impacted by Sunday's preaching, chose to collide with people in their own community in Charlotte. They wanted God to bring revival to their city. They sent requests to Sunday to come back, but it never worked out because of Sunday's failing health. These local businessmen would not be deterred in impacting their community. They met often on the local dairyman's property to pray that God would send someone to their city to preach the good news of Jesus Christ and that He would raise someone to take the gospel around the world.

In 1934, these local businessmen asked Mordecai Ham to hold a revival in their city. During that meeting a young man named Grady Wilson came to know Christ. Wilson was so moved to see his friends come to know Christ he invited them to come the following nights. One night his good friend Billy Frank came with him to the revival and accepted Christ. Because of a burden to impact his friends, Wilson was used by God to bring his friend Billy Frank to Christ. Billy Frank would go on to be known to the world as Billy Graham. Billy Graham has been used by God to preach to more people than anyone else in the history of the world.

So how did the ministry of Billy Graham ever come to be? It was all because a Sunday school teacher decided to have an impact in his students' lives. One relatively unknown man, who lived fifty years before Billy Graham was born, had a passion to engage with others about Jesus Christ. He was neither a pastor nor a professional evangelist. He was simply a Sunday school teacher with a passion for others. He allowed himself to be used by God to have an impact.

As you read this book, I hope you can see yourself as someone like Edward Kimball. You might ask, "How could God ever use someone like me?" God wants to use you to share the hope you have so He can change a person's life. It is not always easy to be someone who tells others about Jesus Christ. Some will reject the message. But, when you share the good news, God is using you to bring that person one step closer to Himself. Perhaps, one day you will lead someone to Christ who will forever change the world all because you took the time to share the hope you have within. Is it scary to allow your world to collide with others? Will some people reject you? Yes. However, these disappointments are so minuscule compared to the joys of impacting someone's life for eternity. My prayer for you as you read this book is that you allow God to shape you into a Collider, someone who is used by God to speak into others' lives.

Will Graham
Billy Graham Evangelistic Association

# PROLOGUE

## A Foreign Land, Recycled Can, and Strange Man

Good-bye icy subzero, eyelash-freezing, Canadian winter! Hello sunshiny, balmy, toasty, Hawaiian beach! Thoughts of snorkeling, sunbathing, and refreshing lemonade in tall glasses with those fancy little umbrellas pervaded my mind as my family pulled into the driveway of our resort condo. My siblings and I (Dan) set aside our bickering from the seven-hour flight and agreed on one thing: the beach wasn't going to come to us.

Dashing into the condo, we chucked our bags into our rooms and in a fluid, unbroken stream of movement threw on our swimming gear, pivoted, and exited through the back door. With nary a glance backward to see if my family was ready, I made the short sprint toward the sandy oasis. It was everything I'd hoped for. Exotic tropical fish zipped around me; warm waves caressed my feet. An hour passed in the blink of an eye. Then my rumbling stomach reminded me I hadn't eaten a thing for hours except airline pretzels. I tossed out the idea to my dad that it would sure be nice if he would bring me a BLT and an icy Gatorade. He suggested a nice tall glass of "get over it" and informed me he'd gone out for groceries while I was sunning myself. So a quick pit stop at our little home away from home was in order.

To my delight I discovered that my parents had crammed the fridge and pantry full of Vanilla Coke and double-stuffed-mint

Oreos. Ahh, inexplicable bliss and gluttony. Much too lazy to change out of my wet swimsuit, I plopped down on the couch, tossed my sand-covered feet onto the coffee table, and switched on ESPN. As I gazed idly about the room, I realized life was good. To my right I could see the waves rolling in to shore. In my lap was a cornucopia of all my favorite junk foods. In front of me was a huge flat-screen TV with a hockey game. And to my left stood a man staring at me, wearing only a towel . . . man *in a towel*?

"Can I help you?" he asked.

*Oh no.* Jumping up I looked down at the Coke-stained, crumb-covered, soaking wet couch. *Oh please no!* My peripheral vision caught a glimpse of my family happily filing into the condo next door.

"Um, actually I was just about to leave . . . uh . . . would you like me to recycle this can?"

## Comfortable but in the Wrong Place?

Dan was happy and relaxed but slightly disoriented—just going with the flow, hanging loose, and having a good time. All it took was a big guy in a little towel to show him he was not quite where he needed to be. It's so easy to get sidetracked when we're not paying attention. We get all settled in only to discover we're in the wrong place. Where are you—not physically but spiritually? Are you where you want to be? Are you where you *need* to be? Or have you been coasting along, unaware of your surroundings? Perhaps this book can be a wake-up call of sorts (but hopefully less mentally and emotionally scarring than Dan's experience) if you have grown a little too comfortable.

## Flickering Flames

There was a buzz of excitement on the bus as our youth group returned from summer camp. God spoke powerfully, and many encountered Him in fresh, unique ways. When Sunday came around, beaming teenagers lined the front of the church auditorium. One after another the invigorated campers eagerly shared how God spoke to them. Several were called to be pastors or career missionaries. Some came to know Jesus for the first time. Others renewed their resolve to live boldly for Christ. The possibilities were endless. The exhilaration was evident to the entire church family. Where would these kids end up? China? Africa? Planting new churches? Representing Christ in the business world? Only time would tell, but we couldn't wait to see how our group was going to change the world . . .

. . . Several years later the scene was much different. Only a handful followed through with their commitments. Some angrily turned their backs on Christ and now lived in open rebellion. For others the falling away was gradual. Talks of attending seminary or starting that Bible group on campus slowly died out, suffocated by endless excuses. Doors opened for them leading them away from God's will rather than into it.

An estimated 70 percent of those who grow up attending church will drop out of church life and in some cases forsake the Christian faith entirely. Most people who abandon church involvement will do so between the ages of eighteen and twenty-two.[1]

The most frequent question we've been asked during the crazy journey of working on this book is, "Why are you writing it?" The answer is: we want to help change those heartbreaking statistics. The Bible says life is a race and we should run to obtain a prize (1 Cor. 9:24–27). However, we've watched in disappointment as many of our peers drifted away and lost interest in the race altogether. Many other young people have settled into a moderate, comfortable jog—still in the race but no longer in contention for that prize. God has shown us life can be so much more than this. We want to encourage our generation not only to stand strong in the faith but also to made a difference in the culture around us!

## Making Our Faith *Our* Faith

This book comes directly from the heart; it isn't prettied up to make us look good. We've included numerous stories of our foibles and antics, which will hopefully give you some laughs. (You're laughing *with* us, right?) But we've also made ourselves vulnerable and shared some of our struggles and poor choices. We hope you can learn from our trials and mistakes as well as some wisdom we've acquired along the way.

We are extremely fortunate to have grown up in a strong Christian family. Since we were young, adorable little boys, godly adults such as our grandparents, aunts, and uncles have continuously demonstrated what it looks like to live in God's power. Our parents took us to church every Sunday and encouraged us to make a positive difference in our community. They modeled and explained the love of Jesus to us. However, as strong as our family was in the Christian faith, our own individual encounters with God gave us a life-changing realization: No one else can live out your faith; that's between you and God.

God challenged both of us to develop our own unique relationship with Him, and He has led us on a fantastic journey. We've traveled to six continents (sorry Antarctica!) sharing with teens, young adults, and senior adults what God has taught us. We've been on numerous mission trips, to some remote places we'd never heard of before, ministering to people in unbelievable poverty and hardship. We've been part of medium-sized and large churches, and we've helped start some new church plants. Recently we were invited to write this book so we could share our hearts with other young adults like you. At the time of writing, we have both recently graduated, Mike from seminary and Dan from university. We are both actively following God's call on our lives to enter full-time ministry. Our sojourn has been beyond what we could have ever imagined—at times terrifying, sometimes heartbreaking, but certainly never boring. We've both had ups and downs and reached places that called for the clear choice to go with God or go it alone, but our experiences have continually propelled us to stay in the race and pursue the prize.

How about you? Are you enjoying a vibrant, personal walk with God? Or are you trying to ride the coattails of your parents' faith? Maybe you're on the brink of bailing out because the Christian life bores you or constricts you. The world certainly has plenty of dazzle to lure you from following Christ. We're going to do our best to challenge you to stay the course, walk closely with Jesus, and let Him use your life to change our generation. Following Jesus is an amazing adventure. Christ offers a joyful, abundant, exciting life that unfortunately many people never experience. Don't be one of those people. Don't be another statistic. We all come to a fork in the road where we must decide to follow the whisper of God or the shouts of the world. Which will you choose? Hopefully by the end of this book, you will have chosen well.

**Part 1**

# PREPARING FOR IMPACT

## Chapter 1

# WHEN WORLDS COLLIDE!

*In every action we take, we are doing one of two things:
we are either helping to create hell on earth or helping
to bring down a foretaste of heaven. We are either
contributing to the broken condition of the world or
participating with God in transforming the world to
reflect his righteousness. We are either advancing the
rule of Satan or establishing the reign of God.*[2]
—Chuck Colson (Christian author)

*Whither is God? I will tell you, we have killed him—you
and I. All of us are his murderers!*[3]
—Friedrich Nietzsche (atheist philosopher)

### See You at the Pole!

Giddy with excitement, we cruised to the video rental store. I (Mike) was twenty; Daniel was eighteen. We had an evening of brotherly bonding on tap. Older and more experienced, I naturally saw this as an opportunity to reinforce my status as the sophisticated, streetwise one. I set out to bring back that 1990s swagger and prove to Dan his big bro still had *mojo*. I glided through the front doors, hooking my shades onto the neck of my shirt, nodding and winking at the other patrons. Dutifully Dan shadowed me a half step behind, no doubt taking mental notes. After we made our manly selection of action thrillers and first-person shooters, we proceeded to the checkout counter.

"It's on me," I assured the kid, pulling out my wallet and flashing several bills. The preteen girls behind us sighed in admiration. As we made our exit, my peripheral vision alerted me—a pretty girl was waving to us from her parked car. This was too good to be true! Now was my moment to shine. *Watch and learn, kid. Carpe diem.* Ramping up my swagger and brimming with confidence, I gave her my TKO combination: the slight nod with the two-finger wave, finishing with my most dazzling smile. *Oh yeah, she totally . . .* SMASH!

When I came to, I was lying on the sidewalk with a supersized headache and the strange sensation of something ebbing out of me. It wasn't blood; it was my dignity vacating the premises. As my world slowly stopped spinning and my vision refocused, I caught sight of the colossal cement pillar I just sashayed into. I staggered to my feet and sheepishly shuffled over to my car where Dan was slouched low in his seat, trying to avoid the appearance of even the remotest connection to me. I slumped into the driver's seat and dared one last glance at the girl. She was laughing hysterically, tears of mirth streaming down her lovely face.

## When Worlds Collide

Life is full of collisions. Do you notice them? Have you seen them? Have you heard them? From microscopic molecules bumping together in a boiling pot of water to clashing galaxies billions of light-years away, collisions are everywhere. Consider conflicts in our culture: two rival sports teams square off in an epic challenge of skill and strength; divorcing couples play emotional cat and

> *Life is filled with spiritual collisions, and our response to them will have far-reaching consequences for both us and the world around us.*

mouse over who gets the house, the car, or the kids. Gangs lock horns in turf wars. Religions feud because they can't agree to disagree. Doritos mixes spicy buffalo and ranch chips in one bag (for which we are eternally grateful). Internal conflicts figuratively and literally tear apart countries; protesters march against the establishment; two galaxies meet to form NGC 731; patients are rushed from highway smashups to hospital trauma units. Collisions are everywhere.

Physical conflict is a fact of life. So are spiritual battles. It's not visible, noisy, or readily obvious, but it's every bit as real. The Bible says collisions are happening in the spiritual realm all around us (Eph. 6:12*). Collisions change everything. Usually there are winners and losers. Physical conflicts call for a response (stay and fight, retreat, give up, get up, and try again). Remaining neutral is not an option. Have you thought about your spiritual life that way? The world bombards you with choices and opportunities and your responses can have significant repercussions, not just for you but for others. In the original *Star Wars* trilogy, Darth Vader and Obi Wan Kenobi engage in a cosmic tug of war for Luke Skywalker's allegiance. He can't stay neutral; he must choose. Not to legitimize the Force (although as kids we tried avoiding several spankings by using Jedi mind tricks), but spiritual collisions happen every day, forcing us to make decisions that shape our lives. From the moment we finally stop slapping the snooze button and crawl out of bed until we hit the pillow again at night, whether we realize it or not, our faith connects with *everything* we do in one way or another. Like the bumper-car attraction at the amusement park, some collisions are directed at us and others we initiate; we can get gently tapped or wickedly blindsided. But if we want to go for the ride, we'd better plan on getting hit.

## One of These Things Is Not Like the Other

According to the apostle Paul, until a person trusts Jesus as Savior, that person is spiritually *dead*, but those who accept God's gift of grace, which is eternal life, are made spiritually *alive*

*For full reference of all verses cited, see "Scripture Reference" section starting on page 207.

(Eph. 2:1–10). Paul further points out that prior to salvation, everyone lives according to this world, which is the devil's domain. Comic strips like *The Far Side* show the devil as the ruler of hell, sitting on a fiery throne with his pitchfork, condemning all the inmates to spending eternity in a cramped cell watching *SpongeBob SquarePants* reruns with their mothers-in-law. But Matthew 25:41 explains that hell was created as a place of *punishment* for Satan and his angels, not as a kingdom for him to rule. So where *does* the devil live and work? The Bible says Satan is the ruler of *this* world (Eph. 2:2). When you became a Christian, God snatched you away from Satan's grip and sheltered you under the lordship of Christ. Enslavement to Satan's domain is no longer your default option.

Numerous Bible verses caution Christians that we are living as aliens in a hostile world, overrun by sin and evil. It may sound like the premise for a cheesy B-movie, but Christians essentially live among spiritual zombies, people who may go to school with us, work with us, or live next door to us, but who are spiritually dead. That's a pretty extreme contrast. Sounds a bit like *Night of the Living Dead* actually. But the reality is, everywhere we turn, we encounter people who are not experiencing the spiritual life that comes from God. They're not "the bad guys"; they don't wear black cowboy hats or sound like a suction hose when they talk, but spiritually speaking, they are fundamentally our opposites. Our two worlds cannot blend seamlessly together. There *will* be collisions.

The world is brimming with people who are adamantly, even violently, opposed to God. Consider atheist Sam Harris's challenge: "If the basic doctrine of Christianity is correct, I have misused my life in the most conceivable way. I admit this without a single caveat. The fact that my continuous and public rejection of Christianity does not worry me in the least should suggest to you just how inadequate I think your reasons for being a Christian are."[4] *Oh snap.* Did you know books promoting atheism have climbed to the top of best-seller lists over the last few years with such champions as Richard Dawkins and Christopher Hitchens actively preaching *against* God's existence? Don't be fooled; the nonbelieving world is not indifferent to Christianity. We should not be shocked when people don't appreciate our beliefs and are even hostile toward God. In fact, if you are a Christian, people all around you hate what you stand for.

So here you are, brought to life through the death and resurrection of Jesus, living in a world that opposes the One who gave you that life. *Your* world is now so different from the one in which you live, a collision is unavoidable. You are like a soldier dropped into enemy territory with the battle surrounding you on all sides. What are your options? Immersed in a world that does not share their values and beliefs, some Christians avoid collisions at all costs. Many simply look for places to hide to keep from clashing their friends, neighbors, and coworkers. Others choose to surrender, giving up the fight and crossing the line into hostile territory waving a white flag. God calls His children to live radically different lives from nonbelievers, but it can be highly intimidating to stand out or stand up for Him.

> **CULTURE CLIP: *THE TWO TOWERS***
>
> In J. R. R. Tolkien's classic book *The Two Towers*, hobbits Merry and Pippin encounter strange tree-like creatures called Ents, living deep within an ancient forest. For thousands of years, the Ents lived out their lives in peace, refusing to believe the news of wars and destruction plaguing the outside world. When the fearful hobbits meet the Ent leader, Treebeard, they plead with him to aid in the war against evil. Although it takes much deliberation, Treebeard eventually realizes the importance his involvement would play in the war. He reasons, "If we stayed at home and did nothing, doom would find us anyway, sooner or later." He agrees to join them and the Ents go on to play an invaluable role in defeating the evil that threatens Middle Earth. (Tolkien 1965)

## They're Coming!

A classic science-fiction book, written in 1932 by Philip Wylie and Edwin Balmer, is called *When Worlds Collide*. (Hopefully that's not the book you *thought* you were ordering from Amazon when you got this one.) In that book, from which we obviously pinched our title, the human race faces a dire situation: two planets called Bronson Alpha and Bronson Beta are hurtling through space, and their paths are leading straight toward Earth. Scientists determine it will only be a matter of time before the planets collide with Earth, utterly destroying it. They realize it is not a matter of *if* the collision will happen but a question of *when*. Many characters in the book try to ignore the imminent catastrophe and carry on living as though there is no danger. But when those celestial bodies appear in the night sky and the seas begin to rise and the Earth quakes, even the most skeptical awaken to the grim reality of what is coming.

It's futile trying to ignore the inevitable. There's no way to avoid spiritual collisions because Christians and non-Christians are fundamentally different beings, like citizens of two different planets.

## Don't Fill in the Blanks!

One night several of us were hanging out together in a public park, cooking hot dogs over a fire, when a handful of teenagers crashed our party. For the most part they were friendly (of the "I've been puffing the magic dragon" variety) except for one outspoken guy who was obviously the ringleader. He was looking for a fight. He began throwing out controversial topics trying to stir up an argument. No one humored him.

When he got to Christianity, out came a spray of profanity about the evils of organized religion. His aversion to the Christian faith was obvious in every four-letter word. Allow us to paraphrase his oration for you: "Christians are (blankety-blank) fools, clueless about (blankety-blank) life. They blindly follow a (blankety-blank) lie and force it down everyone else's (blankety-blank-blank) throats. (Blank.)" The irony was not lost on us that he was the one doing the forcing just then. He went on to threaten us and our mothers and our pets. What caused his venomous revulsion toward God? He was spiritually dead. Eventually our fire went out, and his died for lack of fuel so we parted ways. That night we experienced the blind hatred of a world without God, and it wasn't pretty.

An authentic Christian life *should* incur resistance. In fact, Christians should face *more* opposition than other religions because Satan despises the truth.

What does it look like when spiritual worlds collide? Some collisions (like the one at the campfire that evening) are merely unsettling. Others can be emotionally painful. A friend of ours had a professor, an evolutionist, who scoffed at her stand on creation. He used his superior position to ridicule her continually until she finally broke down in tears in front of her classmates.

Sometimes Christians collide with tragedies rather than personal enemies. Those collisions can be devastating. We live in a fallen, imperfect world, and life can blindside us with some heavy blows.

Brad was a kid in our small town who used to play on the same soccer team we did. He was a gifted athlete who excelled especially at football and basketball. He was also an honor student, highly popular, and came

> *It will not always be the world's treatment of us which results in a collision; it is our reaction to the world.*

from a close-knit, loving family. His parents both taught high school, and his two older sisters adored him. He was a big guy who stood over 6'4". When he was nineteen years old in his second year of college, he was diagnosed in mid October with acute leukemia. He died in early December.

His tragic death shook not only his family and friends but the whole community. The family chose to have his memorial in the high school gym because none of the local churches had the capacity to hold the number of mourners expected. On the day of the service, even the high school couldn't hold the large crowd. People lined the walls and filled every available standing space. His former teammates wore their football or basketball jerseys in his honor. The question on everyone's mind was, "Why Brad?"

He was known as a young man of integrity, recognized as a fair player, a good sport, and a respectful, serious student. He was not obnoxious or pushy about his faith; in fact he practiced a gentle Christianity where his actions spoke for him. Five different clergy stood up, one after another, and told stories about his quiet faith—things he said and did most people never knew.

The family was deeply grieving and shaken but not defeated. His sisters bravely stood up and shared with the thousands of mourners that they were trusting in God to see them through the arduous days ahead. The family asked for prayer. The songs they chose for the service spoke of God's love and kindness. In the midst of the darkest days of their lives, this family presented the hope of Jesus to several hundred hurting and confused teenagers. The world needs to see our faith lived out like that. Often our reactions to the collisions life brings have the greatest impact on a spiritually dead world around us. Unbelievers stand back in amazement when Christians face collisions differently from them.

## The Little Things

My (Dan's) first paying job was at a small, locally owned (and completely sketchy) video rental store. The pay bordered on slave labor, and the environment was dodgy with fights and drug deals going down sometimes just outside the front doors. Once a young man staggered in the door bleeding profusely and asked us to please call the police because he had just been stabbed and didn't feel chipper enough to call them himself.

On weekdays the store was empty. Having already watched all the Disney movies multiple times, we contrived a game to endure the slow shifts. It was called "Case Bounce." The rules were simple.

### Case Bounce 4 Dummies

1.  *Borrow* one bouncy ball from the front-door vendor.
2.  Alternate turns between players bouncing the ball across the room.

3.  The ball must hit the floor once, bounce up, and collide with movie cases on the wall, knocking them off the shelf.
4.  After eight turns each, count fallen cases and crown player with superior numbers the winner.
5.  Repeat until players lose interest or boss returns. Winner keeps the ball.

Being the undisputed intercontinental champion, I quickly discovered that one hard throw at a single case would simply cause the ball to bounce back. However, a series of softer lobs could jostle the cases inch by inch across the shelf. Eventually a domino effect would result, and *voila!* the entire shelf came crashing down. (Disclaimer: if you try this at your job and get fired, I will deny any knowledge of the game.)

The point is that sometimes a series of small blows can cause more damage than a big one. They say it's the little things in life that matter. That's a great line to pull out when you go cheap on your friend's birthday gift, but it also speaks truth on a deeper level. What does God have to do with the little things? It's fairly obvious the two worlds are colliding when someone screams, "I hate God!" in your face, but collisions also occur on a smaller, more subtle level and those add up.

The people in the early church were told to do *everything* for God's glory (1 Cor. 10:31). What would that look like today? Everyday life doles out plenty of opportunities to find out. For example, how do you act when someone cuts you off in traffic? What do you do when a friend betrays you? When your girlfriend or boyfriend cheats on you? When you knock heads with your parents? What is your decision when friends invite you to see a movie you know you shouldn't watch? How do you react as a customer when you are treated disrespectfully? In other words, what happens when things don't go your way? Do you say and do the same thing everyone else does, or do you respond differently? OK, what about when things *do* go your way? What would you do if a cashier undercharged you by ten bucks? Or if your best friend's gal starts giving you a little too much attention?

Lots of people mistakenly view God as only relevant to the big things in life but not the small. However, isn't life actually made up of smaller moments? Conservation experts know that extensive damage happens over years of almost imperceptible erosion as wind and water eat away at soil millimeter by millimeter. The great Dutch painter Vincent van Gogh, when asked the secret behind his masterpiece, responded, "Great things are done by a series of small things brought together."[5] On the flip side, what happens when we neglect the little things? Perhaps Daniel can illustrate.

## Last Skate of a Legend

I (Dan) sniffed the air and a welcome aroma gently caressed my nostrils. Aw, if perfect had a scent, surely it would be thou. Few fragrances can stir such emotion or command such passion as the glorious bouquet of an old hockey bag. Each piece of equipment uniquely perfumes the air: the odor of sweaty shoulder pads bringing back pungent memories of my first childhood game, the scent of mold-infested shin pads rekindling thoughts of glorious victories from years gone by. The time had come, and after a four-year hibernation from hockey, I would return to the ice and recapture my former glory.

Having recently migrated from hockey-crazed western Canada to "if it ain't college football it ain't a sport" South Carolina, I vowed to educate these Southerners on the great Canadian game. Enrolling myself in a local adult hockey league (a.k.a. washed-up collection of has-beens), I arrived at the rink for the first game and confidently marched into the dressing room. Today the prodigal son comes home.

All eyes turned to me; the aura of my veteran presence reeked with authority (or maybe that was my hockey bag). "Boys," I barked. My teammates instinctively snapped to attention. "We'll play a tight left-wing lock, quick D-to-D up-ice transition, aggressive fore-check, then put the biscuit in the basket!"

Stepping onto the ice, I bolted forward, darting around like the Flash. My leg muscles tingled as they awoke from their prolonged slumber, but knowing my team looked to me to set the standard, this warrior battled through the pain.

A burning sensation progressed across my thighs, and sweat rained down my brow, flooding the ice. My legs trembled uncontrollably, yet I still pushed my wobbly body across the ice. *Legends feel no pain.*

Finally, with bile clogging my throat and my vision blurred, I released one last agonizing primeval scream, then collapsed in a disheveled heap. It was over.

Desperately sucking air, my muscles too atrophied to move, I gazed up toward heaven. I could faintly make out Saint Peter beckoning me toward the pearly gates. *Follow the light.*

Just then, in a beautiful moment of brotherhood, a teammate called my name (and was that "Chariots of Fire" playing softly through the loudspeakers?).

"Blackaby. Get up. Warm-up skate is over! Time to start the game!"

*Lord, take me home.*

## Woefully Unprepared

Dan neglected hockey for several years while paying much keener attention to triple-cheese nachos. As much as he wanted to be in the big game, he was kidding himself, to put it mildly, about the shape he was in. He should have learned this lesson ten years earlier. One day when our dad was seminary president, he happened upon Dan (age twelve) lounging in his office chair, his feet propped on the desk, sipping a cool one. He told dad he was practicing for his future. Dad gently suggested that if he wanted to get started on the path to the executive office, maybe it was time for a part-time job. With a lazy shrug Dan replied, "Nah, I think I'll just skip all that menial stuff and go straight into upper management." Unfortunately, that isn't how life works (as Dan and his $6.75/hour eventually found out).

## The Wreckage

Maybe you've seen friends gradually drift away from God because they never got around to taking their faith seriously. They were happy with churchy activities and superficial Bible study, so when their faith took a blow at work or in college they collapsed like a house of cards.

Collisions leave wreckage and they are rarely private. Doesn't it frustrate you to tears when *everyone* slows down on the highway after a car accident? They all want a glimpse of the carnage. It's human nature. A guy in our youth group thought it was no one else's business that he was doing drugs, drinking hard, and partying because he still showed up every Wednesday night for youth meetings. He just wanted everyone to accept him for who he was. But a group of middle-school boys at church emulated everything about him—the way he dressed, the way he talked, and all the bad decisions he made. When it was brought to his attention that he was leading these younger boys down a destructive path, he shrugged and said, "I never asked them to do what I'm doing." But it didn't matter. They were watching him. And he seemed so cool they blindly imitated his destructive choices.

We may never know how far our influence, for good or bad, may reach. But one thing is certain: we don't live in a vacuum. Like a rock

---

### CULTURE CLIP: *THE X-FILES*

A popular science-fiction TV show in the 1990s called *The X-Files* had two FBI agents (Fox Mulder and Dana Scully) investigate a series of unexplained supernatural mysteries. They discovered a vast world of paranormal activity and government conspiracy hidden under layers of secrecy. To their horror, they realized alien life had been planning the extermination of the American population for years. Throughout the series Mulder and Scully embarked on a crusade to expose their discoveries to the rest of the world, but they met with stiff opposition. Interestingly, the resistance came not only from those behind the coverups but also from the general public. Although people refused to believe in a world beyond their known experience, they were nevertheless being influenced by it each day. The more they ignored the world of the X-Files the more it subtly shaped their daily lives.

tossed in a pond, our influence on people ripples out much farther than we may ever even know.

## Two Natures in Conflict

R. C. Sproul wrote, "In one sense, life doesn't begin to get complicated until one becomes a Christian. When we are born of the Spirit we are born anew into a fierce struggle between the old man and the new man."[6] We have a human nature that is vulnerable to this world although we have been saved from its death penalty. Temptation surrounds us, beckoning us to wander from the narrow path for a quick dip into the pool of sin. Don't do it! We have been saved from that world of spiritual death and brought into new life to honor God. When your friend sends you a trashy YouTube clip, ignore it. If your girlfriends are losing weight by purging or starving themselves and you don't like what you see in your own mirror, don't follow their lead. Christians have to stand up and have the guts to be different because God has called us out of this world to live in an amazing relationship with Him. God has much better things in store for us than the world will *ever* offer.

Every time you collide with this world, a part of you will whisper, "Colliding is hard; maybe you should give in just this once." That's the voice of spiritual death calling you back to the grave. Ignore it. Listen to God instead. He promises you abundant life (John 10:10). He wants to give you joy and fill any emptiness in your heart. You can trust Him to do that.

## Little Green Men

One of the greatest products of science fiction is the "aliens come to destroy earth but humans fight back and win" movie genre. *Independence Day* made us all grateful Will Smith is here to save the day if aliens ever pay us a hostile visit. When two worlds meet, a conflict is inevitable. Have you ever seen an alien movie in which the ETs invade our atmosphere, mutter, "Must have taken a wrong turn at Rigil Kentaurus," and fly off into space? No! An epic conflict *always* takes place involving varying degrees of heroism, cowardice, and apathy.

In the film, some wanted to embrace their alien visitors so they stood atop skyscrapers and welcomed them to earth. Those were the first ones to get vaporized. Others fled and sought refuge where they could continue to live in peace. Some of them survived, but they played only bit parts in the unfolding drama. The third group chose a counterposition; they fought back and met the opposition head-on. They were the ones who saved their world. Those three responses actually reflect the three ways Christians can face spiritual collisions, as we'll see in the following chapters.

## Burning Embers

For three days in 1871, the city of Chicago experienced an enormous disaster, known today as the Great Chicago Fire. Gigantic flames raged through the city, consuming the closely adjoining wooden buildings and leaving a death toll of more than four hundred. But even after the fire was extinguished, the area remained too scorching hot for authorities to examine the damage for several days. Although the flames only burned from Sunday until Tuesday, the tragic effects remained for months, years, and even a lifetime.

Collisions in this life have repercussions, and only God knows how lasting those might be. Brad, the guy we mentioned earlier, lived only nineteen years, but the difference his short life made in our town was enormous. Colliding is not about surviving and saving our own skin; it's about impacting peoples' lives.

> We collide with the world so that those who have never seen the power of God can witness Him in our lives.

What spiritual collisions have you experienced? Did your relationship with God grow stronger through those struggles, or did you back away from your faith? How have your decisions affected those around you, for good or for bad? In the next chapters we'll lay out the three potential reactions when worlds collide. We'll look at two not-so-good responses and then turn our focus onto the third one, the one that can make a difference.

Read what Jesus prayed for His disciples. His prayer is the basis for this book:

I have given them Your word. The world hated them because they are not of the world, as I am not of the world. I am not praying that You take them out of the world but that You protect them from the evil one. They are not of the world, as I am not of the world. Sanctify them by the truth; Your word is truth. As You sent Me into the world, I also have sent them into the world. I sanctify Myself for them, so they also may be sanctified by the truth. (John 17:14–19)

## SO WHAT?

1. What collisions are you facing right now? How are you handling them? Identify some obvious and not-so-obvious collisions.
2. How are you keeping yourself strong so you can handle the collisions that come your way? List two or three people you might meet with to pray, friends who could encourage you to stay strong.
3. Has a collision gotten the best of you? What was the damage? What can you do to get back in the game? How could God strengthen your faith through the experience?

## WHAT NOW?

1. Start a journal to record your journey through this book. On the first page, list the biggest spiritual collisions you are currently encountering. Consider how you are handling each one. Then pray over each one and ask God how you can stay strong (and then do what God tells you).

2. Connect with one or two trustworthy friends and pray for each other to stand firm in your faith. Check up on each other through the week to see how each of you is doing.

3. Go to a bookstore or library and get Chuck Colsen's book *How Now Shall We Live?* or Lee Strobel's *Case For Faith* or *Mere Christianity* by C. S. Lewis. Or look up some online videos of William Lane Craig or John Lennox to see some Christian responses to the world's slams against Christianity. These guys will challenge you to think about your faith in new ways.

4. Think about someone you know who "went down" in a collision with the world. How did you respond? Were you critical? Did you gossip? Did you notice? Did you care? Why not reach out to that person and offer some encouragement?

### Chapter 2

# CONCERNING CAVE-INS

*So the difficulties of religion are called trials, because they
try those that have the profession and appearance of saints,
whether they are what they appear to be, real saints.*[7]
—JONATHAN EDWARDS (GREAT AWAKENING PREACHER)

*I don't know if I could go with [Jesus] all the way,
but I could go with Him much further than most
professing Christians can.*[8]
—BERTRAND RUSSELL (ATHEIST PHILOSOPHER)

*They are not of the world as I am not of the world.*
(JOHN 17:16)

## Bears, Stares, and Embarrassing Affairs

I (Dan) had only been at the airport a few minutes, but I had
already checked into the wrong airline and attempted to fill a cup
with ice, forgetting to remove the lid first. I thought the worst was
over. I was wrong.

The line of grumbling travelers at the security checkpoint stretched out interminably. However, my impatience quickly evaporated as several young girls filed in behind me. *Must be a cheerleading squad*, I thought. With the shrewdness of Sherlock Holmes, I immediately deduced from their nervous chatter they were first-time flyers. Puffing out my chest, I muttered, "This line's long but nothing like the lines in Paris. And of course *no* airport is as bad as Chicago O'Hare." I nonchalantly flipped opened my passport, revealing a page riddled with international immigration stamps. I flashed them a confident, reassuring smile, "Just follow me. You'll be OK." They giggled and grinned, obviously impressed to meet a young and attractive world-class traveler.

Occasionally I glanced at my cell phone to check the time and shook my head about the inefficiency of flying. Finally it was my turn to strut through the metal detector. Immediately, a security officer approached me. "Sir, we'd like to double-check your backpack." Reluctantly agreeing, I apologized to the young ladies behind me for this needless delay. "Just routine," I assured them. "Probably need to scan my laptop."

Suddenly a wave of panic washed over me, and I lunged for my bag, but I was too late. The agent found the contraband. He pulled out George, my fluffy brown teddy bear. Chewing the inside of his cheeks to keep from laughing aloud, he gently placed George to one side in open view of the long line of amused travelers as he continued to search my bag in slow motion. I have no idea how the party of pretties behind me reacted because I hurried off "to catch a close connection." George traveled in my checked luggage on the flight home.

Looking back, I smile at the irony of that moment. George was a gift from my girlfriend (now wife) Sarah, a prized possession. He represented the love and acceptance of an amazing girl. But his existence embarrassed me and made me self-conscious when others were watching.

## Embarrassed by Who We Are

How often do similar awkward moments happen as we live out our faith before a watching world? An authentic Christian life flies in the face of what the world around us stands for, so it's easy to see why we might try to avoid uncomfortable conflicts. Like chameleons blending in to their surroundings to avoid predators, we often try to look like the world to sidestep unpleasant confrontations. It's annoying when a situation blows our cover. We don't mind being known as a Christian at church, but we'd just as soon not carry that label around school. Our faith, something that represents our most priceless relationship, becomes the object of humiliation. If we could just look enough like the rest of the world, at least on the surface, and keep our faith safely stowed out of sight, then everything would be much better, right?

We've both been guilty of wanting to hide our faith. Mike was once reading a Christian book for school while waiting in an airport. When a fellow

> **CULTURE CLIP: *THE STRANGE CASE OF DR. JEKYLL AND MR. HYDE***
>
> In R. L. Stevenson's classic tale, Dr. Jekyll is a prominent and highly respected London physician. He is popular and revered as a man of integrity. One day he miraculously invents a potion that morphs him into the hideous Mr. Hyde. A simple antidote reverses the transformation.
>
> Jekyll uses his new alter ego to indulge in all the sin and pleasures of the world from which the respectable Jekyll abstained. However, one night he goes to bed as Jekyll and wakes up as Hyde. In horror he realizes he has lost control of the transformations. In his final speech he laments:
>
> "I began to reflect more seriously than ever before on the issues and possibilities of my double existence. The part of me which I had the power of projecting, had lately been much exercised and nourished . . . and I began to spy a danger that, if this were much prolonged, the balance of my nature might be permanently overthrown, the power of voluntary change forfeited, and the character of Edward Hyde become irrevocably mine."

passenger curiously asked him what he was reading, he shrugged, admitted he didn't really understand the book, and left it at that. It was the truth, for the book flew completely over his head (one of many), but he also missed the opportunity for a conversation about Christianity.

We hope by the way we live, the things we do, and the things we *don't* do, people will somehow just know we're Christians, and this will somehow impact their lives. But the truth is people might never know about Christ unless we tell them.

## Cave-Ins

Growing up in Sunday school in the 1990s, we loved those red blocks that looked like giant bricks. We'd construct epic towers and mighty castles with them. Our favorite thing was to build a fort around ourselves and crouch down inside to hide from the girls (*Ewwww!*). Of course the "bricks" were actually just hollow blocks made of cardboard. They were so light the slightest tap from the outside would send them caving in on us. A Christian life built on compromise is like those blocks; it might look impressive, but it is lightweight and easily knocked over by any pressure from the outside. We become a Cave-In when our weak spiritual shell collapses like the walls of our little cardboard imitation (albeit impressive) forts.

So what causes us to crumble? Sincere Christians don't set out to be Cave-Ins. Most started out with honorable motives. They didn't want to offend their non-Christian friends or appear judgmental. The world loves to play the "holier than thou" card. If that doesn't get the desired response, there's always the trump card: "Christians are so intolerant!" *Ouch!* So well-meaning believers are careful never to offend anyone (except God).

Some churches try hard to look like the world so people will feel comfortable in their building. Is it wrong to try to be relevant or current? Are we *obligated* to sing hymns with titles like "How Tedious and Tasteless the Hour" and "Dwelling in Beulah Land"? Must we pray like time-warped citizens from King James' England? ("*Lord, if*

*Thou dost see fit to maketh that hot guy taketh an interest in me, Thy maidservant, I shall bless Thy name every day Thou givest me breath."*)

The question is, at what point does "blending in" cross over to "selling out"? We heard a preacher lace his sermon with swear words in an attempt to speak the language of any "seekers" in his audience. A seeker-friendly church we know took down the cross and replaced it with the national flag for fear a cross might alienate non-Christians. The Bible certainly doesn't beat around the bush on this topic: *"Adulteresses! Do you not know that friendship with the world is hostility toward God? So whoever wants to be the world's friend becomes God's enemy"* (James 4:4). Pretty strong words. According to James, if we choose the world over God, we declare ourselves to be His *enemy*. Surely the reason many Christians are having no positive impact on the world today is because they have inadvertently sided with Satan by the way they live.

> The reason many Christians are having no positive impact on the world today is because they have inadvertently sided with Satan by the way they live.

## So We *Thought* We Could Dance

A few years ago we traveled to Botswana, Africa, to assist a missionary couple. One particularly unforgettable night we were helping host a college kick-off party. As the students began to arrive, we made an astute observation: we were the only white guys. We stood out like Klingons at a Star Wars convention. Slyly opting out of the basketball game due to our "hereditary weak ankles," we thought we were home free. Then the unthinkable happened, a catastrophic event that would drastically change the face of Africa forever.

"Everybody up, it's time for the dance competition!" *Jesus, come quickly!*

With no place to hide, we were instantly surrounded on all sides by African college students expertly nailing dance moves we only dreamed about. We were trapped! In that moment we did what any other self-respecting, scrawny white guys would do—we started cutting a rug.

Daniel broke into a perfectly executed "sprinkler" dance, flailing around the dance floor like a man possessed. But that was only the prologue. The dance floor split like the Red Sea, and the crowd gasped as Mike dove into a head glide.

Thankfully several of the guests were med students and assured Mike he would make a quick recovery. We were the only ones eliminated from the *warm-up*. As hard as we tried to look like those around us, nobody was buying it.

## Fakes

The outcry was huge when golf pro Tiger Woods fell from grace. Even the secular media roasted him. Was it because he slept with numerous women? Lots of athletes do that and are not lambasted for it. Was the uproar because he was unfaithful to his wife? If that didn't happen regularly among the rich and famous, *People* magazine would be out of business. Had his off-course dalliances affected his golf game? No. The vehement outrage was because he wasn't the squeaky clean family man he pretended to be. Nobody likes a fake. When it comes to celebrities' many forms of expressing their sexuality, the secular press doesn't bat an eye, but nothing hits a nerve like hypocrisy.

> **CULTURE CLIP: GREEN DAY**
>
> The punk legend band Green Day has experienced a lengthy, enormously successful career. Religion has often played a significant role in their music but not in a positive way. "Hypocrites" have been the subject of several bitter lyrics, and in the song "East Jesus Nowhere," vocalist Billie Joe Armstrong rants about those "believers" who dress up in their Sunday Best, although they have long since abandoned their faith into the river of doubt.

Surely nothing galls (or delights) the world more than Christians who act holy on Sunday but live the rest of the week the same way everyone else does. It's something to think about when we are tempted to "blend in so we can witness." Should we wonder when the world concludes: "If their faith is so important, why do they try so hard to act just like us?" One survey in David Kinnaman's book *UnChristian* revealed 84 percent of American nonchurchgoers personally knew a Christian but only 15 percent of them claimed there was a noticeable lifestyle difference in them.[9] When we cave in, those who witness our collapse are turned away from God because He appears irrelevant to our daily lives.

## Summary

In an intriguing *MythBusters* episode, the hosts tested the theory that a house can withstand the onslaught of a tornado by simply opening all the windows and doors. To their surprise it proved true. The tornado passed right through the house, leaving the building standing in its wake. However, when they stepped inside the house, they found it had been completely trashed and hollowed out. The outside looked the same, but the interior reflected the devastating results of letting in the raging storm.

Obviously caving in is not the best way to handle collisions. The next chapter will examine another common mistake Christians make when our faith clashes against secular values. After that we'll look at a different approach that has been God's plan for us all along.

> ### CULTURE CLIP: *THE DARK KNIGHT*
>
> At the onset of the movie, district attorney Harvey Dent is the moral hero of the citizens of Gotham City. They look to him for guidance amid the evil times in which they live, knowing his pure character will see them through. However, Dent's life is altered by a series of tragic events, including severe burns to his face, and he descends into a life of evil. His character radically changes. Or does it? Perhaps the evil was there all along; it was only exposed later. Dent had serious character issues from the beginning, but he hid them well. Trials have a way of exposing one's true character. The burns on his face mirrored the ugliness of his soul now revealed.

## SO WHAT?

1. Jot down your definition of what it means to be a Cave-In. Why do we cave in? What effect does caving in have on your faith? How might your caving in affect other people?
2. If you're keeping a journal, list some areas in your life where you have caved in. Ask God to show you specific ways you can take a stand for Him once again and record those too.
3. Consider why you've caved in to the world. What fears or misperceptions caused you to respond that way? What would need to change in you so you don't cave in anymore?

## WHAT NOW?

1. Make a list of every area of your life where you are tempted to compromise your faith. Keep it in your Bible and pray over it regularly, making notes of your victories and your defeats.
2. Admit what you are doing. If sin has enslaved you, call a minister at your church or seek help from a godly adult who can counsel you. If you are caving in to temptation, determine right now to face your sin head-on.
3. Do you have a friend caving in to the world? Find a caring way to reach out and help that person get back on track. Watch your own heart so you aren't judgmental, and be sure you don't dishonor God in the process.

## Chapter 3

# REGARDING CAVE DWELLERS

*The cross is not just a badge to identify us and the banner under which we march; it is also the compass that gives us our bearings in a disoriented world.*[10]
—John Stott (Christian theologian and author)

*The most important thing about Christianity, from a social and historical point of view, is not Christ but the church.*[11]
—Bertrand Russell (atheist philosopher)

*I am not praying that You take them out of the world but that You protect them from the evil one. . . . As You sent Me into the world, I also have sent them into the world.*
(John 17:15, 18)

### To Nap or Not to Nap? Was There Ever a Question?

I (Dan) fondly recall the summer of 2001. That was the year youth camp became entirely more pleasurable. My friend Rob and I stumbled upon a brilliant observation: the powers that be scheduled recreation time immediately after free time. Well, for us free time always meant nap time. But it was never long enough, and we would no sooner drift to sleep when it was time for chapel. But *now*, by simply not emerging from our cabin for rec, we could grab another hour of shut-eye. The camp leaders at the basketball court would naturally assume we chose soccer instead. The soccer leaders would conclude we opted to try sand art. In short, *no one would know where we were.* It seemed like a foolproof plan.

Furthermore, to our absolute delight, our cabin counselor that year shared our affinity for napping. It was destined to be the best camp experience ever. Until one afternoon we were violently ripped from our slumber by the wail of a fire alarm. Outside, panicked screams were accompanied by hurried footsteps scurrying about. Our youth pastor's voice rang out above the din, begging for order. Our trio's eyes met, but not a word was spoken; we knew what must be done.

Without rising, our counselor reached up to where the speaker was attached to the wall. *Crack!* The alarm rolled across the room and bumped against my cot, the severed wires now useless. He grunted, "Fire alarm's not working," and in unison our heads flopped back to our pillows. Ahhh, what dreams may come!

## Cave Dwellers

In the previous chapter we discussed what Cave-Ins do. But that's not the only possible response to the collisions around us. Sometimes we prefer to find a safe place to hide, free from the voices and pressures of the outside world. Chaos may be ensuing just outside our door, but we closet ourselves away from the needs and temptations out there and choose to remain blissfully uninvolved.

Thanks to a growing Christian subculture, it's becoming easier than ever to avoid the outside world. For just about everything the world offers, there seems to be a Christian alternative. We can get Christian music, movies, books, toys, candy, clothing, video games, and even comic books (we never pictured Abraham with a cape).

We can go to a Christian school, attend a Christian dance class, play on church sports teams, work out to Christian aerobics, hang out at Christian coffee shops, sing Christian songs, and involve ourselves in numerous forms of "Christian culture." But in attempting to insulate ourselves from any and every form of non-Christian influence, we become Cave Dwellers.

We're not referring to hairy Neanderthal men who eat mammoth jerky and choose their wives by clubbing them over the head (now *that's* kissing dating good-bye). We're talking about believers who stay inside the walls of their Christian fortress where they have everything they need: relationships, a social life, common language, entertainment, support, etc. On the plus side these people recognize the harmful effects an ungodly world can have on them, and they are taking steps to guard against compromising their faith. The only problem is, God called His people to make a difference in a decaying and darkened world (Matt. 5:13–16). He did not call us

| CULTURE CLIP: *THE VILLAGE* |
|---|

In this 2004 movie by M. Night Shyamalan, the story follows the members of a nineteenth-century village; they are told horrifying stories of monsters that lurk in the surrounding forest, so nobody ventures outside the village borders. Then a blind girl named Ivy decides to investigate the fearful tales. She discovers a startling truth . . . spoiler alert!

It is, in fact, the twenty-first century. The village is actually deep within a wildlife reserve, secluded from the outside world. The village elders orchestrated a vast conspiracy to escape the harshness of the outside world. They developed a community, mimicking the simpler days of the nineteenth century and invented a lie about monsters so the following generations would never know the truth. In this way life went on for more than thirty years.

In their attempt to protect themselves from any contamination of the outside world, the elders fashioned a "safe place" to live out the rest of their lives in peace. However, they could not escape the influence of human nature, which still pervaded the confines of their secluded village. Reality and its unavoidable tragedy still found them.

to cloister ourselves away from it. Ironically, retreating to a cave can appear to be a safe place to live, but your address will be in a cave. If you live in a cave, the world *has* affected you and has robbed you of much that God intended for you to enjoy and experience.

So what's the solution? Do we opt out of Christian activities and gatherings altogether? Snap all our Christian CDs in half? Burn our Christian books? For the record we are totally in favor of Christians buying Christian books written by Christian authors (for obvious reasons). But Jesus wants us to *influence* the world, not cower from it (John 17:18).

Wilmer McLean was farming near Manassas in 1861 when the American Civil War broke out. The first battle was fought just outside his house, and a cannon ball found its way into his living room. Desperate to avoid the fight, Wilmer sold his farm and moved to Appomattox, Virginia, seemingly far away from the conflict. But to his dismay, several years later the war again found its way to his doorstep. In fact, the peace treaty that ended the Civil War was signed in his living room.[12] No matter how hard we try, avoiding conflict is impossible.

## The Time I Almost Got Away with It!

Early on in school I (Dan) developed an important philosophy: School is not about how hard you work; it's about how hard your teacher thinks you work. I spent years (and several detentions) perfecting my talents, and by the time seventh grade rolled around I was a master; my impressive hours-worked/grades-earned ratio inspired the unabashed awe of my classmates. I soon learned, however, that even great theories are not always fail proof.

Sitting at my desk daydreaming, I didn't notice my teacher start lecturing. One word violently dragged me back to reality, "OK, let's start *presentations.*"

Franticly flipping through my agenda, I found the date. There it was in bold capital letters: ***CLASS PRESENTATION***. Yep, the same one I'd known about for weeks and did absolutely nothing about. I was up second (the curse of having a last name beginning with B).

I took a deep breath, "Stay focused; you can do this." Jeff got up to present first. Just my luck. The dude was president of student council since before I could tie my shoes. He pulled out a homemade shoe-box diorama. My head fell to my desk.

He finished; the class erupted into a hearty applause. I groaned. The moment of truth arrived. I grabbed a blank piece of paper, flashed a fake smile, and winged it.

They laughed, they cried. My speech was perfect! Looking up from my false notes, I saw every eye riveted on me. They were eating it up. I ended with a powerful closing statement worthy of our Founding Fathers and with a humble bow returned to my desk to a glorious symphony of cheers. I made it! Almost . . .

"Excuse me, Dan." It was my teacher. "You mumbled in the middle there, and I missed some information. Can I have your notes to clarify it?" She stood holding out her hand with a victorious smirk on her face. Busted!

> The safe life of a Cave Dweller leaves us ill-equipped to collide with the world.

When we foolishly think we can avoid collisions, we tend to live accordingly, without giving them a second thought. Then, when we are suddenly thrust into one, we find ourselves grossly unprepared. Moments of truth *will* come and the safe life of a Cave Dweller leaves us ill-equipped to collide with the world. Although we may have masked our life to look spiritually mature, an untimely collision will inevitably reveal our true condition.

## Too Much of a Good Thing?

Bats are a highly fragile species. In their caves the temperature and humidity levels remain relatively constant so they haven't acquired the ability to adapt to environmental changes. Like many in Christian communities, they do fine as long as no outside influence invades their habitat, but any disturbance from outside throws them off their groove. The longer one lives in seclusion, the harder it becomes to leave. We can't hide inside our cave and expect to impact our spiritually dead world (Matt. 5:13). The collisions we try to avoid are the ones Jesus spent His time *seeking* (Luke 19:10).

Growing stronger in our faith does not mean saturating our lives with Christian activities or even Christian knowledge; it involves *living out* our faith. The point of Bible study on Sunday is to equip us to collide on Monday. An alarming number of young people fall totally apart spiritually as soon as they leave home. Why? Because many of them spent years so cocooned their faith was never tested. They were unprepared for when they had to leave the safe confines of their Christian world to get an education and a job.

## CULTURE CLIP: CHARLES TEMPLETON

Charles Templeton was a multitalented man. During his life he was a newspaper writer, TV actor, news anchor, magazine editor, best-selling author, cofounder of the organization Youth for Christ, and a Christian evangelist. He was a close friend of Billy Graham, and many who knew him would have picked Templeton to become more famous than Graham. His ability to communicate was unparalleled, and his ministry thrived. But Templeton faced doubts about his faith. He eventually made the shocking announcement that he was renouncing his faith in God. His final published work was titled *Farewell to God: My Reasons for Rejecting the Christian Faith*. In 2001 Templeton died of Alzheimer's disease. Although he spent years of his life in "Christian activity," he died a self-proclaimed agnostic.

## Summary

What do Cave Dwellers and Cave-Ins have in common? Both seek to avoid messy collisions. Both may love God and have good motives, but they are seriously hampered by their misguided responses to the world. Many atheists look at Christians and see people obsessed with appearances or religious activities. Jesus reserved some of His harshest rebukes for the Pharisees of His day, who were known for their religious rituals and hypocrisy. In turn they chastised Him for mingling in the "secular" world.

Often the first thing we do when people become Christians is rip them away from their old life. We plug them into church

> *The point of Bible study on Sunday is to equip us to collide on Monday.*

activities and sign them up for Bible studies, and they soon lose all contact with their former crowd. Their friends are left bewildered, with only the memories of a friendship now lost. Isn't it ironic how we can do this and then spend hours brainstorming new evangelism ideas on how to reach out to people? Perhaps if we didn't so easily discard those friends we already know, we'd have a more receptive audience for what we have to say.

Jesus doesn't tell us to blend invisibly into the world or to hide away from it. Neither Cave-Ins nor Cave Dwellers have a significant impact on people who desperately need to see the love and light of Jesus. To buddy up with the world makes us enemies of God, and to cower from the world disobeys His command (John 17:18). So what are we supposed to do? In the

> *Perhaps if we didn't so easily discard those friends we already know, we'd have a more receptive audience for what we have to say.*

next chapter we'll look at what it means when Christians collide with the world and what can happen when they do.

## SO WHAT?

1. Are you a Cave Dweller at least some of the time? Is most of your life lived within the walls of your church? If so, jot down a few examples of ways you hide away from the world.

2. If you tend to be a Cave Dweller, think about the reasons. Are you motivated by fear? Apathy about those who don't know

Jesus? Are you too busy or preoccupied? Have you simply grown up in the church and this is all you've ever known?

3.  What might it take for God to move you out of your cave so you can make a difference in the people around you? Are you willing to let Him?

## WHAT NOW?

1.  Take time with Christian friends to gather some ideas about how to impact the people around you. Then go out and *do* some of those things. This is not a way to justify going places you have no business going but rather a challenge to step out of your church routine.
2.  Sign up for the next mission trip your church or young peoples' group goes on. It can open your eyes to a world you may not have seen.
3.  This week begin each morning by asking God for the chance to share your faith with at least one person. Opportunities will come, perhaps on Facebook or in a chat room or (yikes!) in person.
4.  Scout out a local ministry to the homeless and try volunteering one day. It might change your life. It will certainly open your eyes.

# Chapter 4

## COLLIDERS

*Some want to live within the sound of a church or chapel bell; I want to run a rescue shop within a yard of hell.*
—C. T. STUDD (CHRISTIAN MISSIONARY)

*Power comes out of the barrel of a gun.*[13]
—MAO TSE-TUNG (ATHEIST DICTATOR OF CHINA)

### A Hero Is Born

It was a dark and murky night, and an eerie fog settled upon our quiet neighborhood. After an evening of video games and cold Tater Tots, my friends Robbie and Caleb and I (Dan) decided to call it a night. Crashing on the floor, we all drifted to sleep.

At 2:00 a.m. the piercing doorbell wrenched us from our dreams. We stumbled to the front door, but the culprit disappeared into the haze. Mumbling about the rudeness of kids, we snuggled back into our sleeping bags only to be disturbed a few minutes later by a second startling ring. This time we dashed outside, certain to catch the guilty party. We peered through the thick air, but the cunning evildoer evaded us again. All seemed lost.

Suddenly the front door burst open, a blinding white light flooded us, and onto the porch a hero emerged. He was the face of justice, the tool of virtue, and ally to the oppressed; he was Mike, clad only in SpongeBob boxers and slippers and wielding a deadly hockey stick. With the burden of the greater good driving him forward, he marched onward and vanished into the mist.

When he returned several minutes later, he merely muttered, "With great power comes great responsibility," and went back to bed. No one really knows what happened in the fog that night; no one dares ask. All I know is the citizens slept soundly and not another doorbell was heard.

## Colliders

What's not to love about superheroes? Not only are they brave enough to wear head-to-toe Spandex; they also have the courage to step out of the crowd and face the enemy while everyone else scurries for cover. In fact, we are often drawn to superheroes not just because of their superpowers but because deep down they are people like us who make a choice to stand up for what is right. This world needs a generation of young people who will collide head-on with the destructive, distorted values of a society that's seriously disoriented to God. People are apathetic, cynical, or downright angry at God. You probably have friends, relatives, classmates, or coworkers who hope that by dismissing your faith they can keep you from challenging their lack of it. Colliders are simply people who value honoring God more than pleasing people (see Matt. 25:21).

What does it look like to be a Collider? Well, when the world tells you to even the score, you choose to show love to your enemies. Instead of promoting yourself, you put others first. The world says, "Life is short, eat dessert first." You say we were made for eternity, but eating dessert first is still a good idea. In other words, in a society that thinks it's all about us, you know it's all about Jesus. Is it any wonder people in the first century scratched their heads in confusion when they witnessed the disciples' lives? Christian Colliders are so radically different from the world people step back in amazement not because they are anything special but because God's power and love shines through their lives. Colliders act in a way that transforms the world around them and points people to God.

On the morning of September 11, 2001, people around the globe watched horrifying replays of hijacked planes zooming like missiles directly into the World Trade Center. The smoke from those doomed structures filled millions of TV screens as thousands of people fled in terror. In a surreal few minutes, both towers collapsed, sending thousands of innocent victims into eternity.

Amid the devastation of 9/11, acts of incredible heroism emerged. Firefighters charged in as everyone else was scrambling out. As streams of dazed and terrified victims flowed down the stairs, a few brave souls headed the opposite way into the carnage, determined to rescue those who were still trapped on the upper floors. The

## COLLIDER BIO: DIETRICH BONHOEFFER

In the morally bankrupt society of Nazi Germany, fear held most Christians back from standing up against the injustice all around them. A German pastor by the name of Dietrich Bonhoeffer, however, was not content to sit back and do nothing.

He condemned the atrocities of the Nazis when few others would. He eventually escaped Germany and landed on U.S. soil, yet his conscience drove him back to his homeland. Although a lover of peace, the dire circumstances in Germany motivated him to join a failed assassination attempt on Hitler's life. Bonhoeffer refused to let the decay of his world swallow up what he believed.

In his most famous book, *The Cost of Discipleship*, he writes "When Christ calls a man, he bids him come and die." He came from a prominent middle-class German family, and all he needed to do to stay safe was silently ride the tide of Nazism. But when Bonhoeffer's faith collided with the world around him, he ultimately fulfilled what he preached. On April 9, 1945, just days before the Allies arrived, Bonhoeffer was hanged in the Nazi concentration camp at Flossenburg.

towers were only minutes from giving way, but courageous rescuers faced mortal danger to save people they didn't know.

## Never Alone

Colliders intentionally take on sin's destructive forces, even if most people are heading the other way. It would be easier to be a Cave-In or hide away like a Cave Dweller, but Colliders choose to go toe-to-toe with the world. Like the outnumbered armies of Middle Earth facing the vast hordes of Mordor in *The Lord of the Rings*, Christians stand as a minority against the powers of Satan as he seeks to control and destroy everything in his path (1 Pet. 5:8).

Christians are on mission to share the good news (Matt. 28:19–20). Jesus Himself warns us it won't be easy, but His promise makes all the difference: "I have told you these things so that in Me you may have peace. You will have suffering in this world. Be courageous! I have conquered the world" (John 16:33).

> *Colliders choose to face collisions when everyone else is running away.*

Dietrich Bonhoeffer wrote, "When we are called to follow Christ, we are summoned to an exclusive attachment to a person."[14] As we live for Jesus, that means He will be right there with us when honoring Him leads us into a collision.

## Stepping Up and Standing Out

When our friend Arlynn was just months from graduating high school, she had an opportunity to collide with some of the ugliness this world can dish out. A classmate came from a dysfunctional home and was socially ostracized at school. He was big enough no one really wanted to take him on physically, so mean-spirited classmates would instead taunt him in public, where they were safe and he was outnumbered. One lunchtime in the cafeteria, they started to throw food at him and hurl insults. The room was full of students. No one did anything. Except Arlynn. She stood up from her seat and shouted, "Stop It!" A hush came over the lunchroom as the crowd was transfixed by her courage. That's what it looks like to be a Collider.

## Young Colliders

The Bible gives several examples of young people who chose to step forward and collide when no one else would. In fact, the Bible records that often the teenagers formed the front line when collisions were coming. For example:

*David.* You're probably familiar with this shepherd boy who became king. The youngest of Jesse's eight sons, David was stuck sheep-sitting in the fields while his brothers went to battle. When the Philistine warrior Goliath, checking in at almost ten feet tall and wearing armor weighing 125 pounds, baited the terrified Israelites, nobody accepted the challenge until David came on the scene. David probably weighed less than Goliath's armor. But he wasn't about to let this goon mock his Lord.

No one wanted to back David up. Would you? His own brothers criticized him, the army ignored him, and even the king said, "You can't go fight this Philistine. *You're just a kid*, and he's been a warrior since he was young!" When Goliath the gargantuan laid eyes on David the diminutive, he too dismissed him as a foolhardy young braggart. However, David had confidence that "all the world will know that Israel has a God, and this whole assembly will know that it is not by sword or by spear that the LORD saves, for the battle is the LORD's" (1 Sam. 17:46–47). And it went down exactly as David called it. David took out Goliath, and God received the credit. This is what Colliders do. They stand up to the world so even mockers see God glorified through their lives.

*Josiah.* David went on to become king, and one of his descendents was Josiah. Josiah was only eight years old when he ascended the throne. He followed a long line of corrupt monarchs, but as a young man he began to seek God (2 Chron. 34:3). Although most of his ancestors rejected God, Josiah determined to break the chain of evil. Sure enough, he rid the land of depraved idol worship and led his people to seek God again. Judging from the string of nefarious kings before him, people probably didn't hold out much hope Josiah would be any less wicked. But God used this courageous young man to lead His people back to Himself.

*Timothy.* Paul was one of the greatest early church heroes. The New Testament contains many of Paul's writings, including his letters to a young friend named Timothy. Actually, Timothy was more like a son to Paul. Paul recognized Timothy to be a young person of integrity. Timothy wasn't a strong guy physically, but Paul knew his heart and saw true potential in him. Paul encouraged Timothy to set an example for others by his faith (1 Tim. 4:12).

> ### COLLIDER BIO: ALEX AND BRETT HARRIS
>
> At age sixteen the Harris brothers grew tired of the low expectations society placed on teenagers. They believed God could use young people to change the world.
>
> They started a blog at www.therebelution.com where teens could encourage one another to do hard things for God. It became one of the most widely read blogs on the Web, launching a movement mobilizing Christian youth to rebel against the myth that teens are freeloaders rather than contributors to society.
>
> The brothers went on to write a book called *Do Hard Things.* Their timely message started a widespread "rebelution" that flies directly in the face of modern misconceptions about teenagers.

Paul was no pushover when it came to taking on mission partners; he held incredibly high standards for himself and likewise expected other believers to stand firm in their faith. So it was significant that he commended Timothy when others around him were seeking their own interests (Phil. 2:20–22). As Christianity was beginning to spread throughout the Roman Empire, there was fierce opposition, but young Timothy stood against the tide to show people the way to God.

*Us?* So why are there not more young Colliders like David, Josiah, or Timothy? Well, as we've already established, it's not easy. Or maybe we're all waiting for someone else to lead the way. We're holding out until our youth group plans a mission trip or our college pastor does all the legwork for a new ministry. We promise to guard the flank if those with a little more expertise man the front line. After all, it's hostile territory out there; we need an experienced leader. However, someone is already leading, urging us to follow: his name is Jesus.

> *If you travel the earth, you will find it is largely divided into two classes of people— people who say "I wonder why such and such is not done" and people who say "Now who is going to prevent me from doing that thing?" —Winston Churchill*

## Drive-By

I (Mike) was a first-year seminary student, spending most of my time either at school or at church or with my Christian friends. It occurred to me my life had little contact with the "real world." My head was being crammed with more and more theological knowledge, but I seemed to be making less and less of a difference for God. I was feeling guilty, so I looked around to see who else I could blame. What was wrong with my college group and my church? Why weren't my friends doing more to reach out to a hurting world?

Each day on my way to class, I passed by a construction crew laying a new sidewalk. One day I felt it—the unmistakable voice of God telling me to do something nice for them. I tried to ignore the gentle nudge, but a few more days went by, and that crew kept frequenting my mind. Every time I passed by them, I knew I should somehow show them my appreciation. But what could I do? I had no money, I had little time, and I was fairly low on creativity.

Then one afternoon it hit me. I was waiting for others to start reaching out so I could follow them, but God spoke specifically to *me*. I was the one disobeying. I was frustrated, yet I was part of the problem, not part of the solution.

I jumped in my car and drove to the work site, growing more intimidated the closer I got. These guys were not exactly easy to approach. What would a group of tough workmen want to do with a preppy, spiky-haired seminary student? What if they cursed me out for interrupting their work? What if they heaved me into the cement mixer? Before I could talk myself out of it, I marched straight to the foreman and blurted out: "Hey there! I'm a student at the seminary down the road and I drive past this work site every day (*deep ragged breath*), and Jesus said to love other people, and I realized I've never taken time to thank you guys for your hard work, so thank you."

I waited for a response. Those few seconds seemed like an eternity. I think the foreman was trying to figure out if I was for real or fulfilling a double-dog dare.

"Well," I stammered, "that's all I wanted to say. I'll just be on my way now." Then a smile crept across his face. He told me his crew had indeed been neglected by everyone on the road. In fact, people were usually impatient with them for causing temporary traffic delays. Emboldened, I asked if there was anything I could do for his crew. He suggested bringing them some water.

> How many times have we done nothing while waiting to do something?

I returned several minutes later with a case of bottled water and shared some encouraging words with the other workers. God used me that day to be different from the world and to show a crew of pretty cool guys that God cares about them and the work they do. And it only cost me $2.85 and ten minutes of my time.

## Our Own Backyard

Comedian Brian Regan does a sketch about the absurdity of two logging trucks going opposite ways on the highway. With a puzzled expression, he observes, "If *they* need logs over *there*, and *they* need logs over *there*, you'd think a phone call would save a whole lot of trouble!"

Similarly, every year our Canadian churches would eagerly await mission groups from the States who would come and help build churches or teach Vacation Bible School. And every summer our church would get two or three American summer missionaries.

But every year our Canadian churches would simultaneously send mission teams and summer missionaries to the States. There are advantages to doing it that way since mission trips are partly designed to broaden the experience of young Christians and expose them to other cultures. But one summer our church youth leaders did the unthinkable: they planned the annual mission trip right in our own town (the audacity!).

An outcry ensued. Several students debated whether they would even sign up. How boring. But before long everyone rallied around the idea. They planned and organized and set up camp in our church basement. One of their main projects involved a local community of mobile homes, an unwillingly center of controversy. A developer bought the property where these people lived and gave them a few months to relocate. If they were not gone by August, their homes would be bulldozed. The problem was most of them had nowhere else to go. That was the only mobile home park in our town. Several of them were elderly. Many lived below the poverty line and could not afford to hire anyone to help tear down their porches and dismantle their fences. So our church teenagers did it for them. They showed up every day with their work gloves and labored in the July heat, helping wherever they were needed. The residents were astonished and grateful. The local paper sent reporters and photographers. The front page carried their pictures and recorded glowing praise from the relieved residents. Several of the teens were quoted sharing that they were just "loving their neighbors" as Jesus told them to do.

We've been fortunate to join God at work in many places around the world. However, we've also learned that missions do not always require us to brave the dense jungles of South America wielding a machete in one hand and an Evangecube in the other. The call to be a Collider is not an obligation to sign up for all twelve of your church's mission trips. It's about acknowledging the countless chances to make a difference where you live, right now.

One of our friends once snapped at the slow cashier at a gas station, frustrated because we were going to be late for the church bus.

Ironically, the bus was taking us on a mission trip to share the love, joy, and forgiveness of Christ. Every time we go to work, get served at a restaurant, sit beside an atheist classmate, or run errands, we have the opportunity to display and share the love of Christ. The people we pass on the way to our church's outreach event are just as important to God as the ones attending the event. God's plan to spread His good news around the globe does include missionaries, but it also includes every one of us, right where we are. If, as the Bible says, we are no longer part of this world, that makes everywhere we go a mission field since the world is now a foreign land to us.

## No Collisions (or Bad Guys) in Heaven

When we were younger, our action figure collection always needed a healthy supply of "bad guys" (otherwise, who would our Teenage Mutant Ninja Turtles fight?). During one of many epic battles between good and evil that transpired in our basement, I (Mike), being older and wiser theologically, broke some hard news to Dan. "Daniel, did you know there will be no bad guys in heaven? I guess we'll just have to bring our own!"

There will be no collisions in heaven; that's why it is so crucial to collide now. In heaven we will live in harmony with one another and with God, but that isn't the case now. God cares too much about the world to shield us from colliding with it. We need to show people how to love God and love one another. In his work *The Republic*, the famous philosopher Plato used the analogy of humanity being chained together and trapped in a cave, facing a wall where all they see are shadows of the outside world playing out like a hazy puppet show. Having never been outside the cave, the people think the shapes moving across the walls *are* reality. One day a person is released and led outside where he discovers a vivid and colorful new world. He realizes what he saw before was merely a weak representation of something so

> There will be no collisions in heaven; that is why it is so crucial to collide now.

much better. Now what should he do? Run off to explore and enjoy his newfound happiness and forget those left behind? He could. The people back in the cave may doubt him and call him crazy anyway. Or he could go back into the cave, tell the others of his amazing discovery, and help lead them out of the cave to enjoy the same new world.

A Collider, who has received a brand-new life through Christ, walks back into the shadows to help others experience new life too.

## But These Guys Have Mustaches!

We both played inline hockey in our teens. I (Dan) was the team's goalie. Midway through the season we had the dubious distinction of being the league's only winless team (an honor that curiously held true with *any* team we played for). One particular game a vanload of our players was stranded several miles from town, leaving us only a single substitute. To make matters worse, we were playing "The Purple People Eaters." They never lost. They were also known to dine on the flesh of their unfortunate victims.

---

### CULTURE CLIP: "COUNTRY OF THE BLIND"

H. G. Wells's 1939 edition of his short story tells of Nunez, a mountaineer who falls down a mountainside into a valley only to discover a village resting at the base.

Cut off from the rest of the world, the citizens formed a self-sufficient society. However, disease spread among them, causing them to lose their sight, until the entire village was blind. As generations passed, the word *sight* was slowly forgotten.

Nunez tries to explain to the village all the things he sees, but they believe he's simply crazy. Eventually they conspire to pluck his eyes out and put an end to the madness.

As Nunez flees up the mountain, he sees a landslide headed straight to the village. Realizing he is the only one able to see the danger, he heroically returns to the village and saves many people before the avalanche erases the village from history.

As we inched nervously out of the dressing room, we saw them warming up. They towered above us as they whizzed past, performing perfectly executed drills. Our teammate Patrick discreetly shuffled back to the dressing room to throw up. I heard Mike's shaky whisper behind me, "We can't play these guys. They have *mustaches!*"

> A Collider . . . walks back into the shadows to help others experience new life too.

The whistle sounded to begin the slaughter.

The arena suddenly became a gladiator coliseum, and the death toll promised to be high. The People Eaters tossed our players around the rink like rag dolls. From my position in goal, I could see my pale-faced brother who, as the coach's son, pulled rank and was the lucky one to "ride the pine" for the first shift. As Patrick dragged his bloody, mangled carcass on all fours toward the bench, I closed my eyes: *Lord, if it be Your will, please allow my brother to keep all his limbs!*

Mike jumped over the boards and raced into the action. Heading straight toward the opposing team's largest and hairiest player, he did the unthinkable—he threw a body check. The purple behemoth staggered, momentarily stunned, before swatting Mike away like a fly. But I watched an amazing transformation. Our small and grossly overmatched team began playing their hearts out. Each time a beaten warrior would stumble back to the bench, our sub would eagerly jump over the boards to enter the fray. My teammates were relentlessly knocked down, but they kept jumping back up.

When the buzzer rang to end the game, a silent and shocked audience sat staring at the scoreboard which read: Purple 2—Blue 11.

Christians can sit comfortably in our churches, following God's activity through church newsletters and cheering on our pastors and missionaries. Or we can join the action. Colliders choose to get in the game and take the hits. We have to realize simply becoming a Christian doesn't win the battle any more than signing up for our hockey team won us a game. It's a daily commission.

## Misconceptions

We've said lots about what colliding looks like, but it's equally important to clarify what colliding does not look like:

*Conflict.* We once heard a guy sing his pastor's praises saying, "Anyone with that many people mad at him *must* be doing something right!" Jesus said, "By this all people will know that you are My disciples, if you have *love* for one another" (John 13:35). There's a big difference between colliding with the world and just butting heads with it. Jesus never acted like a jerk. Neither should we.

*Big.* Not all collisions will be big or even painful. This world can be a lonely depressing place for some people, and sometimes a Collider simply brings joy to the sick, the elderly, or the lonely. Our mom often travels to a small town to visit her sister who lives in a nursing home. One day she was painting her sister's nails and decided to spread the joy around to the other residents. Before long the room was filled with laughing, white-haired ladies getting manicures. Sometimes our mom will take a puzzle or board game and sit in the common room to spend time with whoever shuffles in. Mom would not be caught dead giving a speech in front of a crowd, but she loves those elderly people. She says it's not a big deal; she enjoys doing it. Jesus said it *is* a big deal: "Whatever you did for one of the least of these brothers of Mine, you did for Me" (Matt. 25:40). We are not responsible for

> Do small things as if they were great, because of the majesty of Christ, who does them in us and lives our life, and great things as if they were small and easy because of his almighty power. —Blaise Pascal

what everyone else does, but we *are* accountable for what *we* do (Eccl. 12:14). Mother Teresa of Calcutta, the tiny nun, said, "If you can't feed a hundred people, then feed just one."

*Believing.* Some people think *believing* in colliding is the same as colliding. The apostle James talked about that. He said: So what? Even demons believe (James 2:19). Our little dog Chevy likes to sit on the front staircase of our parents' house and stare out the window at passing traffic. Any time he sees a car go by, he barks his guts out. However, he can't be heard from the street, and we've never seen anyone so much as look in his direction from their vehicle. But Chevy thinks he's protecting our entire household with all the noise he makes. Some people like to make a lot of noise in church about how horrible the outside world is. Meanwhile the world is passing by their church, heading to an eternity without God, while the noisemaker drones on inside the safety of their sanctuary. At a certain point we need to close our mouths and let our actions reveal what we really believe.

We don't collide because we have some sort of grand vision to change the world; we collide because it's unavoidable as we live a genuine Christian life. By the way we love, the joy we give, the way we serve, our good attitude, our humility, and our passion for Jesus, we will collide head-on with a world that does not understand what is so different about us.

---

### CULTURE CLIP: *TWILIGHT*

Stephanie Meyer's *Twilight* saga is perhaps one of the hottest book crazes ever. It centers on a family of vampires, the Cullens. Unlike other vampires around the world who feed off the lives of humans, the Cullens vow not to harm mortals, substituting animals instead at great cost to themselves.

This decision draws curiosity, puzzlement, and even resentment from the other vampires who don't understand this unselfish decision. The Cullens's father even practices the profession of a doctor, healing and caring for humans while his fellow vampires prey on them.

---

### But It's My Day Off

I (Dan) spent a summer in Athens, Greece, helping feed and encourage refugees. On a day off, I decided to pamper myself and enjoy a luxurious island day cruise. Soon after the ship departed, I met Katie, a sweet fifteen-year-old from Holland who was touring Greece with her mother. As the two youngest passengers, we made a pact to stick together. We spent the day together adventurously exploring the islands (and even winning the traditional Greek dance competition).

She seemed fascinated to learn I was a Christian and my reasons for being in Athens, and she asked lots of questions about it. When the boat docked that night and we were being shuffled back on the bus, Katie made a surprising revelation, "Today was great although I didn't much enjoy all the old churches because I'm an atheist." She added, "But you're cool, not like the other Christians I know." My mind immediately scrolled back, wondering if I'd done anything "cool" for the wrong reasons. It's funny, looking back on that summer I realize one of my most significant encounters occurred on my day off.

## Standing Out

Christians are called to stand out from the crowd. As far as he knew, our friend Caleb was the only Christian on his high school's basketball team. Despite pressure to fit in and the temptation to focus only on winning games, he made a commitment to kneel and pray before each game. His befuddled teammates noticed. As the season progressed, several team members joined him. When his team took the court for the Championship Game, his coach turned to him and asked, "Caleb, could you lead us in a prayer?" Before a jam-packed crowd of friends and family, the team bowed their heads and Caleb prayed. Caleb was pumped about that and later told us all about it. After a while we realized he hadn't even mentioned the score of the game (they won), because for Caleb the victory happened before the first whistle.

Colliders stand out because they let God's love flow through them to a world desperate for a kind word, a bit of encouragement, or a consistent role model. How about you? Is a conversation cleaner when you join in? Do the gossipers avoid you because they know you won't join the backbiting? Can that socially awkward classmate count on you to be kind to her? Are hurting people drawn to you when they need encouragement? Don't kid yourself. The people around you *do* notice what you say and what you do. Getting people's attention isn't hard; any quirky character with a gimmick can draw a crowd (Lady GaGa anyone?). But being noticed for the *right* reasons takes character.

Wars are won where the conflict is, not at boot camp. Colliders stand out because they get into the battle for the right reasons.

## Red

Not long ago I (Mike) had an unforgettable experience. I'd been noticing more and more verses in the Bible about helping the poor. But what could I do? I was a student and considered myself to *be the poor*. It was all I could do to buy food, books, gas, and way too much Diet Coke. But one Saturday morning God convicted me the *truly* impoverished people in my own city were flying under my radar day after day. I made a commitment: that day would be different. I jumped in my car and headed downtown.

After walking all around Raleigh's city center and seeing no one in need, I was discouraged. My attempts to engage (or even find) the poor resulted in nothing. I offered up a frustrated prayer. "God, I believe You led me here; please show me why." Right then I almost bumped into a ragged man pushing a shopping cart of possessions. He was obviously homeless. He immediately greeted me as if I were expected. I asked him if he would like to get lunch, and thus began a memorable afternoon spent in the company of my unexpected new friend named Red.

I gave him a Bible from my pocket, a scarf from my car, and ten bucks from my wallet. I shared some of my story but mostly listened to his as I pushed his cart and we hung out in the park. When it came time for me to head home, he asked me for a ride and I agreed. It proved challenging to fit his cart of belongings into my little Honda, but with the help of a bungee cord and my intermediate skills at Tetris, we were soon on our way.

I dropped him off, and as he thanked me, he pulled out a necklace from inside his shirt. It read "I Believe in Angels," and with tears drawing lines down his grime-streaked face, he pointed to me. "You are the one I prayed God would send to me. You're not like others," he said, referring to those he told me about who dropped money in his palm to ease their conscience and then hurried away without uttering a word to him or looking him in the eye. As he walked away, pushing his cart and fading from my view, I thought about just how much like "the others" I had often been. That memorable day and Red's gratitude will stay in my mind forever.

Jesus obviously had a soft spot for the down-and-out. He was never embarrassed to be seen with them or afraid to talk to them. He ate with them and defended them to their critics. Impoverished people don't just need money; they need the love of Jesus Christ. He's the only one who can truly give them hope. And that Saturday I learned firsthand about something else Jesus gives the poor. He gives them dignity. That was an eye-opener for me. So often *I* was the annoyed or indifferent passerby. As I crawled into my warm bed that night, I wondered where Red might be sleeping at that moment. As the temperature continued to drop outside, my tears finally ushered me to sleep.

## The Challenge

People around you need to see that life holds more than they are experiencing. They need to know about the abundant life God wants to give them. Don't sell out like the Cave-Ins. Don't try to hide like the Cave Dwellers. Now is the time to begin colliding with the world! Let's show them what joy really looks like, what grace feels like, how sweet forgiveness is, and what love really means. Let's show them how awesome our God is! The world may not *want* Christians to collide with them, but they *need* us to. So what does it look like to be a Collider? In the next few chapters, we'll explore some of the biggest collisions we will inevitably face in life and how a Collider meets them head-on.

## SO WHAT?

1. Think of a time recently (in the last week) you collided with the world and people saw Jesus in your actions. How did that make you feel? What resulted from your decision to collide?
2. If there wasn't a time you collided last week, what does this tell you? What's holding you back?
3. Would you say people know you are a Christian by observing the way you live? If not, what areas in your life can you begin changing today?

## WHAT NOW?

1. Why don't you and a friend take a trip downtown and see if there is a homeless person you could take for lunch? Don't hand over money for the meal. Go along. Or pack a picnic to sit and share with someone who is lonely.
2. Think of someone on the outer circle of your group. Take time today to reach out and befriend that person.
3. Instead of sitting in church for your usual Sunday school lesson, your class could assemble little gift bags of candy and take them door to door in your church's neighborhood. No come-to-our-church propaganda; just let them know you're "loving your neighbors" like Jesus said. Don't be surprised if God opens up opportunities for you to talk with them further about Him.
4. On a holiday such as Thanksgiving or Christmas, wrap up a few hot turkey meals and deliver them to people who don't have the day off—such as firemen, policemen, gas-station employees, or nurses. Resist the temptation to hide a tract in the mashed potatoes; just talk openly with them about the love of God and how much you have to be thankful for that Thanksgiving (if you are a Christian, that is a lot).

**Part 2**

# COLLIDING WITH YOUR FEARS

## Chapter 5

# ON A COLLISION COURSE WITH FEAR

*The act of cowardice is all that matters; the emotion of fear is, in itself, no sin.*[15]
—C. S. LEWIS (CHRISTIAN AUTHOR/APOLOGIST)

*It [religion] comes from the bawling and fearful infancy of our species, and is a babyish attempt to meet our inescapable demand for knowledge (as well as comfort, reassurance, and other infantile needs).*[16]
—CHRISTOPHER HITCHENS (ATHEIST AUTHOR)

### Space Mountain (and Why It Still Gives Me Nightmares)

A four-year-old boy is limited in the rides he can experience at Disney World because of the height restrictions. For me (Mike) that was fine, but my thrill-seeking father had other ideas. We had already "conquered" Fantasyland, and if he had to spin in one more teacup, cram his 6'2" frame into another Dumbo, or listen to another stanza of "It's a Small World," he was going to snap—people were going to get hurt. All day he patiently endured every kiddy ride in the park, but enough was enough. After trading in his life savings for our admission, he was determined to get his money's worth. After all, this is the same man who tried to save a buck by asking the ticket agent at Universal Studios if there was a *discount* for being, and I quote, "a decent human being." You don't know 'til you ask, right? Turns out, there isn't.

Drawing on masterful powers of manipulation, he said Mom deserved a break in a coffee shop while he "took Mike on some rides at the other end of the park." She was delighted, and we were gone in a flash, my seven strides matching every one of his.

As we entered an area of the park I never saw before, I noticed a dramatic demographical shift. For starters, there were few kids my age. In fact, it seemed more like a Hell's Angels convention than the Mickey Mouse Club. We pushed ourselves into a line outside the infamous Space Mountain roller coaster, and my big brown four-year-old eyes took in the frightening scene around me. I wasn't the only one having second thoughts, either. Dad, who had not actually *ridden* it since he was a teenager, was beginning vaguely to remember just how spine-chilling that beast could be. He nervously attempted to comfort his terrified little boy.

The *rush* of the roller coaster boomed in our ears, and my dad leaned down and assured me, "Don't worry, Mikey, it's not as bad as it sounds." We made our way within sight of the loading zone. One child, at least eight years old, was wailing hysterically and begging his mother to take him away from that dreadful place. Dad said, "Don't worry, Mikey; it's not as bad as it looks."

A teenage boy, oblivious to my terror, hurried us into the car, one in front of the other, and my dad made a last desperate promise: "Michael, if we get through this, I'll buy you a pony!" Once we were buckled in, Dad reached his big hand onto my shoulder. Even though I couldn't see him behind me, I could feel his hand.

The next few hideous moments carved a permanent scar in my memory. I can still recall the demented, high-pitched screaming, the breakneck speed, and the absolute, utter darkness. All the way through that twisting, turning, tortuous torpedo of a ride, my dad kept shouting out to me that we were almost at the end and reminding me about that pony.

When we finally jerked to a halt and they peeled us out of our seats, Dad quickly knelt down in front of me, checking for any damage. Here was our special, father-son moment. Here was when he told me how proud he was of his firstborn. Now was when he would look me in the eyes and tell me what a brave little champion I was.

"Mike," he pleaded, "no matter what happens, don't tell your mother!" So much for that pony.

As paralyzing as that maniacal experience was, it launched me on an exciting journey. I developed a passion for roller coasters, and now I can't get enough of them. Now *I'm* the one convincing Dad his rheumatism can hold out for one more round on Space Mountain. That induction into the exhilarating world of stomach-churning suspense forever erased the appeal of It's a Small World.

## Wherever He Leads

Everybody is scared of something. It may be spiders (Mike), moths (Dan), or your mother before her morning cup of coffee (Mike *and* Dan). Some fears are substantial like dying, making a speech, launching a career, being alone, losing a loved one, or obeying God's will.

*Obeying God's will?* How scary can it be to read the Bible, show up at church, and say our prayers? God loves us and wants what's best for us so He'd never ask us to do anything that frightened us. Would He? Would He lead us on a journey that might make us completely abandon our comfort zone? Or ask us to do things that seem way over our heads? Our grandfather used to tell us, "Nothing is more exciting than living your

> *Nothing is more exciting than living your life for God. But if what He asks you to do doesn't scare you half to death, you're probably not hearing Him.*
> —Henry Blackaby

life for God. But if what He asks you to do doesn't scare you half to death, you're probably not hearing from Him."

From the early church Christians down through the generations, believers have been called to collide with the world. Sometimes that can be a highly intimidating venture. We can feel like a young Mike, sitting bug-eyed on that roller coaster, about to be hurtled out into the abyss (figuratively speaking). But Jesus has promised to be with us (Matt. 28:20; Heb. 13:5). Colliders throughout history have one thing in common: they trusted God. They knew God led them, and they felt His hand even if they couldn't see Him. Just as our dad wanted Mike to experience an exciting (albeit frightening) new adventure, so God wants to free us from our fears so we can live the awesome odyssey He has in store for us. Yes, God will ask us to do some pretty scary things. Fear can immobilize anyone, but we have a Champion who knows exactly what we'll miss if we let our nerves sideline us. God wants to take us right through our trepidations to collide with our fears and come out the other side victorious.

## Shrinking in the Spotlight

We've both held the not-so-secret dream of becoming rock stars for as long as we've been playing music. Several years ago things began falling into place. We threw together a band with some friends to take part in a small talent show for our church, and we enjoyed it so much we explored the idea of becoming a real band. We recruited a couple more friends and formed Fading Rebel, a rock band that would melt your face off! We eagerly signed up for a Battle of the Bands, and to our delight (and surprise) we placed first that night and began a tantalizing musical journey that would last the next several years.

All five band members were Christians, and given some of the sketchy places we played (beggars can't be choosers), we recognized the chance to share the message of Jesus in a scene that can be ambivalent about God or downright hostile.

During our first few shows we included a brief "God Talk" near the end of our set to share the hope we have in Jesus—nothing too preachy but definitely laying our faith out there. In those early days we mostly played locally, and we had a pretty sizable group of loyal Christian friends who faithfully attended our gigs. Our Christian testimony always drew cheers and applause from them. We felt pretty good about the positive message we were projecting. We wanted to be a light in those dark places so we decided to make those God Talks a regular feature at our shows.

But then we started to get more opportunities to play farther away from home. We performed in surrounding cities too far for our friends to drive, which meant playing to audiences of strangers. No more cheering during our God Talk. This was a perfect opportunity to step out in boldness, but instead we were gripped by fear.

We were playing to head-banging audiences and sharing the bill with hard-living bands so we wanted to avoid doing or saying anything to invoke a negative reaction, as in getting booed or beaten up. We thought by not drinking at the bars or using profanity during our shows we were presenting a good Christian witness. We had promised ourselves we would keep Christ at the center of our music, but when we surveyed those crowds of skeptical, disenfranchised teenagers, our focus became more about not getting heckled and less about sharing Christ's love. The God Talk quietly disappeared from our shows.

There we were, our world butting right up against a world of nonbelief and scorn, and our initial zeal for sharing the hope of Christ gave way to fear and embarrassment. Most of the people in the audience probably never thought about stepping foot in church, but *we* were in *their* world. We wanted credibility with

> We are afraid of colliding because it costs us something to collide.

the crowds. We wanted the other bands to invite us to join their gigs. And we sure enjoyed the crowd's applause. But we risked losing those things with a religious spiel. So we caved in by clamming up.

## Caving In to Fear

Chameleons are intriguing creatures even if lizards gross you out. They're known for their ability to change color to blend in with their surroundings. It's true; some species actually are capable of becoming yellow, brown, pink, orange, green, black, blue, or aqua. But scientists who study the species say the camouflage effect of their color morphing is only part of its purpose. They also change hues to communicate with other lizards. For example, a female chameleon will shut down a potential male suitor by turning red. Or a male will get blue to warn others off his turf. Some biologists say the "hiding from predators" part emerged as a secondary function, with social communication being the primary reason for the color morphing. Whatever the case, that sounds a lot like our band. God gave us the means to communicate with other young people like us and the talent to show them what mattered to us. But instead we used our musical ability to blend into our surroundings. We became indistinguishable from the other bands playing in the same venues. Thankfully, God pulled us back together, and at least for our final show we were able to share our hope in Christ to a roomful of people.

*We rarely think of the cost other people pay because of our inaction.*

Have you ever been a part of a group harassing someone at school? Maybe you weren't participating in the bullying, but you weren't standing up for the victim either. You felt uncomfortable; but, not wanting to become a victim yourself, you silently waited out the humiliation, perhaps even laughing along with the tormentors. Do you have memories of illegal or immoral stuff happening in your presence, times when you lacked the courage to challenge the activity? Did you convince yourself that because you were not actually participating you weren't guilty? Being a nonparticipant or a bystander is really just a passive form of caving in. While holding your tongue may save *your* skin, it won't help those being mistreated. We rarely consider the cost other people pay because of our inaction. A man named Martin Niemoller said this about the atrocities he witnessed at the hands of the Nazis in World War II: "First they came for the Socialists, and I did not speak out because I was not a Socialist. Then they came for the trade unionists, and I did not speak out because I was not a trade unionist. Then they came for the Jews, and I did not speak out because I was not a Jew. Then they came for me, and there was no one left to speak for me."[17]

We're *not* suggesting you should constantly be on the prowl for a fight. You don't have to stash a superhero cape in your backpack in case you stumble across a case of injustice. But moments come in every person's life when you *know* the right thing to do and the only thing holding you back is your timidity. Then the temptation is to mind your own business or play it safe. Yet by your inaction you become part of the problem, and your fear may cost someone else even more than it hurts you.

> ### COLLIDER BIO: DAVID WILKERSON
>
> The last thing on this skinny country preacher's mind was reaching gang members in New York City. But when he came across a picture in *Life* magazine of seven teenage boys charged for murder, God called him to leave the comforts of his world to invest his life in NYC. Walking by faith, David entered the streets of New York in 1958 and began a career of reaching inner-city gang members for Christ. The world of teen violence, sex, and drugs was foreign and terrifying for David, yet God used his life to save many souls and start several ministries. Read his amazing story in the book *The Cross and the Switchblade*.

## Home Run!

Trapped! Four sinister walls enforced my imprisonment. I (Dan) furtively eyed the door, but the warden's eyes were riveted on me, gauging my every move. All around, my comrades were likewise slaving away under the scrutinizing observation of Mrs. Shepherd. Then it happened. She turned her head momentarily, and I realized my opportunity. "We have nothing to lose but our chains!" I cried as I sprinted out the door, down the hall, and into the fresh air of freedom. Thus begin my life as a first-grade dropout.

No more rock-hard desks. No more stiff color-coordinated outfits cruelly forced upon me by my mother. Instead I spent a glorious afternoon doing what I pleased, prancing around in Spiderman briefs and playing Super Mario Bros. Surely this was life as God intended. But alas. My adventure was aborted as I was unceremoniously dragged back to school the following morning, accompanied by a stern warning from my father, and I quote, "If you run home again, you will get the biggest spanking of your life" (a thought-provoking statement considering some of my previous spankings were measured on the Richter scale).

However, during an especially dry lecture on "The Alphabet," I decided it was time for Houdini to work some more magic. Humming a few bars of Alice Cooper ("School's Out for the Summer"), I made my move. Like a swift fox zipping across a stream on the protruding rocks, I pounced up on my chair and pranced in a serpentine fashion across other desktops toward the door. I dove out into the hallway, softening my landing with a shoulder roll. Moments later I breathed the welcome fragrance of fresh air and freedom.

Arriving home a few minutes later, I was surprised (and slightly horrified) to find my frowning father standing in the doorway, phone to his ear and a stern look of disappointment on his face. Suddenly his prophecy about corporal punishment flooded my memory with all its ramifications. Gulping, I flashed a sheepish grin, hoping his bark was worse than his bite. Oh sweet agony, my dad is a man of his word.

## Frightened into a Cave

One way to deal with fear is selling out to avoid scary collisions. A second option is retreating to safety. Sometimes this can seem like a more noble response. At least we don't compromise our beliefs, lower our standards, or go along with the crowd. Best yet, we never have to face our fears. It's like handling a heights phobia by never climbing higher than the front porch. Any time things get dicey, we can rush back to our "safe zone." Or we just don't go out in the first place.

Most Christians consider church to be a safe haven. Our Christian friends there don't put us on the spot about our beliefs or mock our Christianity. We connect with them and speak the same language. So we spend as much time as possible with other believers in situations that won't challenge our faith. When we have to venture out to secular places for school or sports, we scoot back to our church group as soon as we can. We're like rabbits bolting out of their burrows to collect food, anxiously looking about in case a fox is nearby. We grab what we need to live and scurry back to safety.

Have you heard people say, "I'll do whatever God asks me to do except _____"? Or, "I'll go anywhere God sends me as long as it's not Africa."

> **CULTURE CLIP: *CHARLOTTE'S WEB***
>
> In E. B. White's classic tale about farm animals, Templeton the rat spends his time hiding during the day and only emerging at night when he can most easily avoid unwanted encounters with others. White explains, "He had tunnels and runways all over Mr. Zuckerman's farm and could get from one place to another without being seen." Although Templeton's skills and resourcefulness could be of great help to the other farm animals in times of need, he preferred to play it safe by avoiding the dangers of the outside world. By playing it safe, he was of no use to anyone else.

In other words, I'll follow Jesus as long as He takes me where I want to go. Jesus doesn't play that game. He says to take up our cross and follow Him (Matt. 16:24). There are no exemptions given for places we might be afraid to go. He is not our Lord if we never do what He tells us (Luke 6:46). The truth is, if you follow Jesus for long, He will inevitably ask you to do something you are afraid to do. The Bible is full of examples of God calling people out of their comfort zones in order to obey Him, and this usually meant facing their fears.

## Colliding with Fear

*Peter.* When Jesus beckoned Peter to leave his fishing boat and follow Him, He provided no details. He simply said, "Follow Me" (Mark 1:17), and Peter did. What would it mean for Peter to leave the security of a home and a familiar job to accompany a leader who was basically homeless? How would Peter provide for his family? What would Jesus expect him to do? Peter wasn't a public speaker, a scholar, or a theologian. He was trained to catch fish. He was simply minding his own business by the Sea of Galilee with no aspirations to change the world. Peter would make some devastating and costly mistakes along the way, even bailing out on Jesus to save his own skin (Matt. 26:69–75). But ultimately God would use Peter to heal the sick, raise the dead, and preach to crowds of thousands. It wasn't the safest life he could have lived. But what a life!

*Gideon.* The Israelites needed a valiant leader to deliver them from their oppressors, and Gideon wasn't even on their radar. He had zero credentials as a warrior and was certainly not jockeying for the job. Gideon (justifiably) felt totally inadequate to lead his people into battle, but that's exactly what God had in mind. He was the youngest member of the nation's weakest family. The opposition had a massive army and had already proven to be first-class bullies. Poor Gideon was living every day in trepidation, hiding from the Midianites and constantly looking over his shoulder, ready to head for the hills if he encountered the enemy. He was not hero material. Yet God chose white-knuckled young Gideon to lead the charge against the dominant opposing army. Not only that, but then God downsized the Hebrew army from thirty-two thousand to three hundred. But He gave Gideon a promise more powerful than swords and spears and far more forceful than Gideon's fear. "I will be with you," He said (Judg. 6:16). Those words made all the difference. Gideon's army annihilated the Midianites, and Gideon grew to become the leader God wanted him to be.

*Esther.* Esther was an ordinary person, a prisoner of war, in fact, until she caught the eye of the king. She was suddenly thrust into comfort and luxury. Then one of the king's officials, Haman, became furious at Esther's cousin Mordecai for refusing to show deference to him. In retaliation Haman convinced the king to annihilate all the Jews in the kingdom. If Queen Esther played it safe, she would live but all her friends and relatives would die. But if she spoke up, she could end up joining her people on the gallows because anyone, including the queen, who dared approach the king to voice displeasure risked immediate execution. No matter what Esther did, the risk was enormous, and thousands of lives were at stake. Esther chose to stand up and made plans to collide with the royal court. She decided, "I will go to the king even if it is against the law. If I perish, I perish" (Esther 4:16). Not only did she survive that encounter, but God also used her to save thousands of lives.

Peter, Gideon, and Esther worked through their fears to become part of God's miraculous and exciting work. Others include Miriam, David, Jonathan, Samuel, Daniel, and Mary. All of these people had valid reasons to fear for their lives if they accepted God's assignment. But each of them counted the cost and chose to collide with their godless society. The Bible records the astounding results.

## Just a Spoonful of Sugar, or Was That Baking Soda?

I (Mike) am the first to admit there are many things in life I'm not good at, which include (but are not limited to) mechanics, math, and anything outdoorsy. But when the overwhelming thought of baking cookies popped into my head one day, I figured the Aspartame in all those Diet Cokes had finally made me crazy.

I knew God wanted me to love my neighbor in the general sense of the word. But I started praying for God to show me some specifics. It was a simple prayer, and God gave me a simple answer: bake cookies for your next-door neighbors. I'll admit I would have preferred something with a little more testosterone, but the idea persisted.

I'm bad at baking. To this day the only cookies I know how to make are from a recipe on the back of a peanut butter jar (cup of sugar, half a cup of PB, an egg, and "Poof" cookies). But with so many people deathly allergic to peanuts, I decided not to risk killing our neighbors. So I enlisted the help of my sister, promising her a substantial amount of the dough if she would help (works every time).

As the two of us approached our neighbor's house with our slightly burnt offering, it occurred to me how little I knew about them. We lived beside this family for awhile, yet the only conversations we shared were brief moments while shoveling the snow from our driveways. We rarely even saw anyone outside their house. The closer we got, the more second and third and fourth thoughts I began having. I felt like a Girl Scout marching up there with cookies. We walked up their front steps and rang the doorbell. Seconds passed.

"Oh well, we tried. Let's go home." Then the door opened a crack. "Yes?" It was the wife.

I cleared my throat. "Um, hi there. We just wanted to come and bring these cookies over for you." It sounded better in my head.

She slammed the door in our faces and called the police. No, of course she didn't! She was delighted. We exchanged a bit of small talk about snow-shoveling techniques, and then Carrie and I went home.

The next day mom told me our neighbor dropped by that morning to return the plate and chat for awhile. As it turned out, the previous week had been one of consistent bad news next door, including a huge financial setback and the death of her husband's brother. In addition, she shared that she had just recently been diagnosed with OCD (obsessive-compulsive disorder) which explained why she so rarely left her house. She knew lots about our family just from observation, and the fact that two busy teenagers would even care about her apparently encouraged her immensely. That began a friendly relationship between the two households that continued until we moved a few years later.

## Summary

God calls us to step out and collide with our fears. That may involve traveling to a distant land, or sometimes it may just mean baking cookies and walking next door. But whatever God may ask, doing it is always worth the effort. We have no idea what's going on in people's lives around us or who may need the encouragement that will only come if we swallow our fear. What is the cost to ourselves and others when we play it safe? We encourage you to recognize your fears and then learn how God wants you to face them. In the next chapter we'll discuss some specific fears we all encounter and look at the amazing things God can do in and through us when we allow our worlds of faith and fear to collide.

## SO WHAT?

1. List five things that scare you. Then review the list, considering what you may have missed out on because of these fears. Have any of them caused you to "play it safe" and disobey what God told you to do?

2. Why do you think God would ask you to do something that might embarrass you? Why doesn't He just have everyone do what they are good at?

3. Think of the Christians whom you most admire or who have had the biggest impact on you. Consider what it may have cost them to become the men and women who inspire your respect. Do you think they always played it safe?

## NOW WHAT?

1. Think of at least one thing you know God wants you to do that you have been afraid to do. Maybe it's to reach out to someone in need or to share your faith. Maybe you owe someone an apology. Make a commitment right now to obey God, and do that one thing as soon as possible. Watch and see what happens when you do. How did it feel? What did God do in that situation?

2. If you are a part of a Christian group, plan something you could do together that will take you outside your comfort zone and force you to face your fears.

3. Think of a fear that has kept you from following God whole-heartedly. Write it on a piece of paper (use code if it's private) and stick it somewhere visible (like in your car or on your bathroom mirror). Every time you see it, ask God to release you from that bondage. As your week goes by, take note of opportunities God gives you to face that fear and watch how He helps you overcome it.

4. It's therapeutic to face your fears. If you are afraid of snakes, wrap one around your neck and keep it there for five minutes. Just kidding!

## Chapter 6

# WHEN COLLIDING SCARES YOU TO DEATH

*Seeing that a Pilot steers the ship in which we sail, who will
never allow us to perish even in the midst of shipwrecks,
there is no reason why our minds should be overwhelmed
with fear and overcome with weariness.*
—JOHN CALVIN (CHRISTIAN THEOLOGIAN)

*Men are swayed more by fear than by reverence.*
—ARISTOTLE (GREEK PHILOSOPHER)

### Things that Scare Us Silly

In this chapter we'll explore three specific fears everyone struggles
with: stepping out into the unknown, encountering rejection, and
failing. These fears have the power to take anyone down in a collision.
However, God can give us the strength to conquer them. Let's kick
things off with a special guest appearance by our little sister Carrie.

### Fear of the Unknown

*3 . . . 2 . . . 1!*

I (Carrie) was finishing up a three-week marathon trip with my
dad to Singapore, Malaysia, and Australia. We had just arrived at our

final stop in New Zealand, and while my dad checked us into the hotel, something caught my eye. Posted beside the check-in counter was a flashy advertisement for bungee jumping. Now I would by no means call myself a daredevil. In fact, I'm the type of girl who insists on buckling my seat belt just to drive to the mailbox and back. But for some bizarre reason, in my fifteen-year-old naivety I thought, *Why bring home a tacky made-in-China souvenir from my trip when I could have the experience of a lifetime? Wouldn't bungee jumping be the perfect way to end the trip?* Of course, not too long after that I would be considering just how abruptly bungee jumping *could* end the trip, but my mind was made up.

Finally, on the day we were scheduled to fly back to Canada, I found myself overlooking a 154-foot cliff. I was connected to the platform with nothing but a rope lazily looped around my ankles. And frankly it looked thin enough for flossing teeth. I'd never been more terrified in my entire life. My heart was pounding an unsteady rhythm in my chest, and my stomach felt so queasy I feared my lunch might make a second appearance (and it hadn't even been all that tasty the first time).

As I stood trembling with my toes against the edge, staring down the cavernous depths to the river below, the girl in charge patted me on the back and said in a thick New Zealand accent, "Well mate, the longer you stand up here looking down, the harder it gets. I'll count 3, 2, 1, then just go for it!"

3 . . . *sweat sweat* . . . 2 . . . *rattle rattle gasp* . . . 1 . . . ahhhh! (Read in a high-pitched, blood-curdling, glass-shattering, dogs-barking, spine-chilling, raise-the-dead tone.) As soon as I jumped headfirst, I felt a huge rush of adrenaline and then pure excitement. It was one of the most incredible experiences of my life! Not only was it a blast, but it also shamed my wimpy older brothers into trying it a year later.

### Stepping into the Unknown

One of life's most terrifying aspects is the unknown. We remember playing video games when we were younger (OK, so we still play them). Our great discovery was online walk-throughs. These are step-by-step instructions written by experienced gamers (with way too much time on their hands) who have figured out how to beat the game. Every time we encountered an obstacle too difficult to pass, we would simply get online and find the answers. Don't you wish life was like that? The problem is, we can't just jump on Wikipedia and figure out what the future holds. Surely that's why horoscopes are popular; they supposedly take the guesswork out of daily living. But the reality is, hard as we may look, there's no *Walk-Through to Life* (at least, not a good one) sitting on a shelf somewhere at Barnes & Noble.

As badly as we want guarantees about the future, we don't know what kind of news awaits us tomorrow or what challenges the week may bring. We draw closer to high school or college graduation and panic (or at least our parents do) because we have no clear plan in place. Our grandpa always says, "God does not call you to a *career*. He calls you to a *relationship*." That's so true. God may lead you through several jobs in your life (in fact, most college students change their major about seventy-eight times), but you will *always* be called to a relationship with God

> ### CULTURE CLIP: *INDIANA JONES AND THE LAST CRUSADE*
>
> There is a classic scene in this movie where Indy must pass several tests riddled with deadly traps. The final test requires him to step off a ledge into a deep abyss. He does so only to realize there's been a natural rock bridge there the entire time. The walkway, however, perfectly blends into the rocks of the walls around it, forming the illusion that it isn't there at all.
>
> It was a step of faith that even made Indiana Jones sweat with fear!

that involves trusting Him to lead you where you need to be. The scary part is relinquishing control. For all Carrie knew as she stood on that bungee platform, they hadn't even attached the cord to her leg securely. We do the same thing every time we step onto an airplane. We haven't seen the pilot, and for all we know, there is no pilot up there at all but a robot. But one thing is for sure: if you don't trust the pilot, you will never fly because *you* sure can't fly an airplane (unless you happen to be a pilot reading this, in which case, just go with the metaphor).

### Facing the Future

We had a friend who was naturally good at everything he tried. And he was brilliant. His grades could get him into any college he chose. His proud dad urged him to apply to the best schools in preparation for a prosperous future. His teachers encouraged him the same way, steering him toward a lucrative career. In their exuberance they approached the process just as the world would—without God. Our friend followed all the advice against his own second thoughts. It wasn't long before he flunked out of university and had to return home. But through that setback he learned a valuable lesson about following God's plans. This time as he prayed and asked God for guidance, he was led in a completely different direction. Today he is happily on his way to completing a college degree, and his faith has never been stronger.

Following the world's agenda without consulting God is a Cave-In way of making decisions. Cave Dwellers refuse even to entertain the possibility God might lead them away from their comfortable life. The thought never crosses their mind that God may call them to be a missionary or enter the ministry. And even if God *did* lead them to missions, their parents would never allow it.

> Where is God leading you today? How you respond today will determine where you end up tomorrow.

We have both messed up enough times to know what our best planning usually amounts to. Now we strive to follow God's lead. He knows the future, and we can trust Him to carry us into it. Do you want to avoid needless frustration? Follow God where He leads you each day, and in ten years you'll be exactly where He wants you to be. By the way, that place is always best.

## Fear of Rejection

### *"I'm Actually a Cool Guy, I Swear!"*

Ducking into the doorway, I (Mike) saw that only two seats lined each side of the aircraft. I dislike flying, especially in small planes. My window looked directly out onto the propeller. Fear gripped me.

I plopped into my aisle seat and got adjusted; then I heard a soft voice. "Excuse me, I think I'm the window seat beside you."

"OK, just a sec, I . . ." My sentence trailed off. Before me stood a girl who must have leaped straight from the cover of *People* magazine's "40 Most Beautiful People in the Galaxy" edition.

"So, can I get to my seat?" I realized she was still waiting in the aisle for me to move.

"Um, yeah, sure," I stammered, dropping my book and getting tangled in my iPod headphones as I struggled to unfasten my seat belt. Cursing myself for being so inept, I finally spilled into the aisle, and she eased her way past me into her seat.

| COLLIDER BIO: BILL WALLACE |
| --- |

Wallace, a gifted doctor, had an unrelenting passion to share the gospel with the people of China. But it would mean giving up a life of guaranteed luxury in America. Shortly before he was to move to Asia, he was offered a much sought-after partnership position to practice medicine in an atmosphere of tremendous resources and wealth. That would be greatly tempting for any physician, but Wallace had been recruited by God, and nothing would deter him. He declined the offer.

One day a group of guards burst into the hospital where Wallace practiced as a missionary doctor. They falsely accused him of being an American spy, and evidence planted in his room condemned him. He was dragged to prison where they beat him and brainwashed him almost to insanity, trying to elicit a confession. After one such session Wallace closed his eyes for the last time.

Obedience to God cost Bill Wallace his life, but it was a price he willingly paid.

"So, what do you do?" I stuttered.

"I'm just finishing up a year as Miss America Rodeo Princess." *Sweet mother of mercy.* Suddenly I couldn't get my lips in sync with my brain.

"I'm allergic to horses," I blurted. *'I'm allergic to horses?!' That's the best you can come up with?!*

"That's too bad. Do you fly much?"

"Yeah, but I'm terrified of flying." *Mike, what are you doing!? Tell her you play the drums!* "But not as much as I'm scared of spiders! Ha, ha . . . ha?" *Stop It! Honesty is* not *the best policy!*

She gave me an awkward smile, "Don't worry. I'm sure there's no reason to be afraid." I groaned inwardly and slumped back in my seat. This would be a long flight.

### Afraid of Rejection

Why are we so paranoid people might accidently stumble upon the *real* us? We freak out and try to recover anytime we let something slip that doesn't match our manufactured persona. The desire for acceptance can be all-consuming. High school is an especially fierce gladiator arena for people pleasing. What is peer pressure if not a lie to convince teenagers to exchange their values for a temporary membership in the "cool crowd."

We expend far more energy worrying about what people think of us than they spend even thinking of us at all. What if I sound stupid? What if I say the wrong thing? What if my mind goes blank? Too many things can go wrong! I'd better just not say anything and play it safe. Many of the greatest Colliders in history were those who did the right thing at the expense of popularity. They figured out popularity is a fickle thing, and it's impossible to please everyone anyway. If we seek acceptance in the world instead of approval from God, we will end up as a slave to the whims of others.

### My Friends Call Me Batman

My phone rang, interrupting my sleep. Answering it, I (Dan) was greeted by the barely recognizable sobs of my friend Tracy. She lived in the dorm but was house-sitting a large country estate for a friend. *Something must have spooked her,* I thought. "Just wait, Tracy, I'll come by."

Opening the front door, I called out, "Tracy, I'm h . . ." I was cut off by a blood-curdling scream, "For the love of all that's good and holy, *shut the door*! Don't let any more in!" Quickly slamming the door, I spun around; there stood Tracy, white as a ghost.

"*Something* flew past my head," she stuttered. Assuring her that she was merely letting the fright of being home alone get to her, I gallantly offered to inspect the house, just to reassure her.

I looked in every room—no sign of the mysterious winged trespasser. Tracy eventually agreed she must have just imagined it. But walking back to the kitchen, something didn't seem right. We glanced up at the entryway.

There was an ear-piercing, high-pitched, girly scream. I think Tracy yelled too. Hanging by its feet was a mammoth, hairy, sinister-looking bat. I'd seen people walk dogs smaller than this creature. Tracy looked at me and screamed three haunting words, "Daniel, do something!"

Grabbing a stool and a tea towel, I prepared to enter into mortal combat against my fuzzy opponent. I gazed into the blood-red eyes of horror personified, then glanced down at the threadbare, tattered cloth in my hand. "What am I thinking? This monster is huge! It could eat me whole!"

Deep breath. I reached out and seized the critter. He was my prisoner. I sprinted with Olympian speed toward the door. An epic battle of Man vs. Beast ensued. A wing broke free from my grasp and started flapping against my face. The bat's high-pitch shrieks were drowned out only by my even higher pitched shrieks. Finally reaching the door, I flung it out and watched the devilish creature fly off into the night. All in a day's work. The next day Tracy bought me a Batman T-shirt which I proudly wear to this day.

### Jesus Never Promised a Comfy Life

We tend to think that because God loves us He must want us to be comfortable. Somewhere along the way Christians have bought into the assumption the world revolves around us and God spends His time from sunup to sundown thinking of new and creative ways to keep us happy. Well, that's something we have to get over. God has bigger plans for us than simply a soft, undemanding life. He does want us to experience an *abundant* life (John 10:10), but He also wants our lives to change the people around us. Tracy's fear caused her to lock herself in a half bathroom. She was in a beautiful spacious manor, but the only place she felt safe was in the smallest room in the house. Why? Because she didn't know what was out there. That's what fear does. It backs us into a corner of paralyzing inaction. The fear of rejection can effectively turn us into silent bystanders rather than agents of influence in God's will. That's no way to live life. A life spent cloistered away doesn't leave much of a mark on the world either.

## Fear of Failure

### "Don't Be Afraid" (Mike's Story)

I was in my final year of high school, and I had no definite plans for postgraduation. Throughout my life I considered doing many things when I grew up, but one thing was for sure: I did *not* want to be a preacher! Public speaking scared me to death. However, as graduation loomed, I found myself drawn to the local seminary. They had just launched something called the Samuel Program for graduates who wanted one year of biblical foundation before continuing their education, wherever that might be. Hesitantly, I signed up at the last possible date.

The first two weeks went pretty well. It was an amazing atmosphere. As I rubbed shoulders with students from all over the world and soaked in the teaching of the professors, my Bible knowledge grew by leaps and bounds. Yet my heart wasn't in the right space. I felt uneasy because all was not right between me and God.

Along the way something else began to happen. I started feeling more and more tired and run-down. It was understandable since I was working a part-time job at a local coffee shop and carrying a full load of classes. But when I started to lose more and more weight off my already slim frame, others began to worry. My fatigue came to the point I did little outside of school or work other than sleep. My clothes hung from my shoulders like from a hanger.

The third week into the semester was Spiritual Emphasis Week, which meant we attended chapel every day to hear a guest preacher. That year brought a speaker named Jeff, but I wasn't interested in hearing him. It was easy to make up excuses for skipping, so I missed the first two days. But on Thursday something changed.

---

### CULTURE CLIP: BABE RUTH

Babe Ruth is arguably the greatest player in the history of baseball. His swing was textbook, and his dedication to the game legendary.

Today his legacy lives on as one of baseball's home-run kings. He's one of only six players to eclipse the six hundred home-run plateau. Ruth ranks third all-time with an astonishing 714 knocks, and he held the single season record for over a decade.

What is often lost amid his jaw-dropping numbers is that he long held another record too . . . most strikeouts. In his career, he whiffed on the ball 1,330 times! That's almost twice for every home run!

Ruth's attitude was simple. "Every strike brings me closer to the next home run."

Today it's safe to say when people hear the name of Babe Ruth, no one associates it with strikeouts.

---

I was on my way out the door when I felt as if God grabbed me by the shoulder. I was so preoccupied with everything else in my life this spiritual encounter stopped me in my tracks. It's hard to explain, but in that moment I knew I *had* to go to chapel that day.

I found a seat near the back on the edge of a row. Then Jeff started speaking, and every word he said seemed to be pointed directly at me.

He preached from Exodus 14 where the children of Israel crossed the Red Sea. As the Israelites stood at the edge of the water, I clung to the edge of my chair. All hope seemed lost as the water blocked their path and the murderous Egyptian army closed in behind. Why would God take them to such a dangerous place? Had they not been following His will? Why would He lead them into such a hopeless foxhole? Then Jeff said something I will never forget. He said, "Sometimes God sets us up for a miracle so we have no choice but to trust Him. He never takes us around our fears; He takes us through them." You know the rest of the Bible story. God saved the Israelites, leading them miraculously through the sea as He parted the waters on their right and on their left.

At the end of the message, Jeff gave an invitation to anyone who needed to make things right with God. To this day I can count on one hand the number of times I've gone forward to make a decision or to pray at the end of a service, but that day in chapel was one of those times.

> *God never takes us around our fears; He takes us through them.*

I made my way to the front and bowed before God. Tears flowed down my face and with them the stranglehold I had on my own life. I finally realized what I had been fighting: fear. I was afraid God might call me into full-time ministry, and that scared me to death. I would do *anything* to avoid speaking in public. I closed off my ears to God's voice for fear of what He might ask of me. Yet, as I poured my heart out to God at the front of that room, I realized something amazing. I understood God had been preparing me my whole life for this. He *created* me for this purpose. But how could God use someone as ordinary as me? Thoughts like this had bored their way so far into my heart I forgot a simple truth: it is not about me; it is all about God.

As I knelt before God that morning, I could hear Him in my heart simply saying, "Do not be afraid. Trust Me." Then and there I committed myself no longer to live my life in fear but rather to seek God's path, wherever it would take me. My worlds were colliding, and this time I wasn't running. The relief and joy that spread through me at that moment can't be described. You must experience it for yourself. All I know is the Red Sea in my life finally parted.

I eagerly attended the final service the next day. At the close of the service, the president (who also happened to be my father) gave one final word. He said, "God has spoken to many of you this week. God never speaks without a reason. Some of you may not get through this weekend before you discover why God told you what He did." With that, I grabbed my bag and made my way to the door. That's when my dad stopped me in my tracks. He informed me my mom had scheduled a doctor's appointment for me since my constant fatigue started to worry her. There are few things in life I hate more than going to the doctor. But I knew my mom wouldn't budge on this one.

I sat in the doctor's office with a foreboding that something was really wrong. They took some blood samples and sent them to the lab. When they returned, my fears were realized. The doctor said the glucose level in my blood was off the charts and I needed to head immediately to the emergency room. The shock didn't even have time to set in as we rushed home to pack an overnight bag and then hurried to the hospital.

> God knows what we will face tomorrow; that's exactly why He asks us to trust Him today.

Further tests confirmed the bad news: I had Type 1 Diabetes. I had always despised needles, and I was now learning I would be giving myself shots several times a day for the rest of my life. There is nothing one can do to prevent the onset of Type 1. It just happens. I received the worst news in my life, and there was nothing I could do about it.

I didn't get my own room until around 2:30 in the morning. As I laid there alone in my bed with nothing but the blinking lights and quiet humming of hospital machinery around me, many questions raced through my head. The biggest one was, Why would God allow this to happen to me right after I decided to trust Him and do what

He told me? Then it hit me. God knows what we'll face tomorrow; that's exactly why He asks us to trust Him today. As I surrendered my fears to God, He knew the next day I would be tested like never before. I would face the most frightening experience of my young life, and He knew I was unprepared for it. He saw the collision coming, and He made sure I was ready.

This is what it's all about, isn't it? What's the point of faith if it's never tested? God was not taking me around my fears; He was leading me *through* them. I'd thought trusting God only included my future career plans, but it involved much more—trusting God and seeking His will is for *all* areas of life since fears come in all shapes and sizes (and legs, if you have arachnophobia).

> A fear of failure is simply a lack of faith that God will pull through.

When your worlds collide, you must be firmly planted in God's will if you want to come out victorious. When I decided to follow God's will for my life, it included a lot more than simply agreeing to enter the ministry. Was it going to be easy? My medical news proved it wouldn't. Was it going to be worth it? Eight years later (and counting) I can confidently say "Yes." Traveling the world, completing two degrees, preaching, teaching, playing music, and writing a book for God's glory were not even on my radar back then. But when we give our fears over to God, they lose the power to hold us hostage.

### Think Big!

An old French proverb says: "*Il qui craint de souffres, souffre de la crainte.*" (He who fears to suffer, suffers from fear.) Our excuses ("I'm too inexperienced, young, uneducated, shy, busy, broke," etc.) may get us out of doing what God tells us to do, but we're the ones who suffer the lost opportunities. When we pull out our list of shortcomings, we're really just expressing our doubt that He has the power to work through us. Even worse, what if we step out in obedience but He's not there for us? How do we know He has our backs? Here's what God said through the prophet Isaiah (41:10): "Do not fear, for I am with you; do not be afraid, for I am your God. I will strengthen you; I will help you; I will hold on to you with My righteous right hand." God may make you face some scary situations, but always remember He is right there with you. Exercise your faith. God didn't teleport the Israelites across the Red Sea *Star Trek* style. They had to trust with each step He would keep those walls of water on either side from collapsing on them.

Do you ever get tired of having a small view of God? Step outside tonight and look up at the stars. Those are the same stars Abraham gazed upon when God promised to establish a great nation through him. The sun that beat down on David's back as he approached Goliath is the same sun that brings out your freckles in the summertime. Every single story you read in the Bible features, as its main character, the same God you serve today. Let's keep that in mind the next time we want to tell God "I can't" because what we are really saying is "I won't" or "God can't." If God has called you to do something, don't fear failure because if God can create an entire universe from nothing, He can surely help you face whatever collisions might lie before you.

### Lighting Their Candle

As you may have noticed by now, the two of us have contrasting personalities. However, moments in life come where differences must be put aside and an alliance formed for stark necessity of survival— like our family vacations. We love our family, and we deeply appreciate much about our parents. However, we often clash over the idea of what is fun. Our father has a Ph.D. in history. He gets a buzz from seeing a historic roadside marker and salivates at the thought of walking through an old graveyard (which is slightly creepy). We, on the other hand, prefer to see old castles that repelled violent sieges and weapons wielded by noble knights (boys will be boys).

Several years ago we took a vacation to England. The place is crawling with old buildings and cemeteries. To our dad it was

El Dorado! In Oxford we could hardly keep up with dad, who kept skipping merrily through the streets in search of something ancient. Eventually, tired and slightly embarrassed that Dad looked like a giddy Joe Tourist, we stealthily gave him the slip and headed to a tourist shop to find something a little more "King Arthur" and a little less "Church History Greatest Hits."

Suddenly dear old dad, gasping for breath, appeared in the gift shop doorway, "Come here quick!" He bellowed. "I found it!"

Not knowing if he'd discovered an all-you-can-eat buffet or the tomb of Henry VIII, we reluctantly followed. Abruptly he stopped in the middle of the crowded courtyard.

"See. It was right here!" he announced. We had no idea what he was talking about. Just as we were starting to suspect he had accidently stumbled into an English pipe shop, he explained.

During the 1500s, the Protestant Reformation took place in England. People began a return to vibrant, personal relationships with Christ. Two of the leading ministers who spurred this change were Hugh Latimer and Nicholas Ridley. These were saintly men, known for living upright and holy lives. Then a new queen came to the throne. She didn't earn her nickname "Bloody Mary" for nothing. She was violently opposed to the new teaching and preaching of men like Latimer and Ridley. They were warned by their friends to head for the nearest cave or they could be in big trouble. But they stuck with their convictions and were soon arrested by Queen Mary's henchmen. On October 16, 1555, the two condemned men were taken to the courtyard in which we now stood. The executioner, wanting to make sure these men were *really* dead, built two enormous stacks of firewood. Latimer and Ridley were each tied to a post in the middle of the wood and given a final opportunity to recant their unpopular beliefs. The men declined. The fires were lit.

A great crowd gathered to watch these two devout men suffer an agonizing death. When the flames began to leap around Ridley's head and his courage began to wane, his good friend Hugh Latimer shouted to him amid the din, "Be of good cheer, Master Ridley, and play the man, for we shall this day light such a candle in England as I trust by God's grace shall never be put out!"

. . . "Two good men died right here 450 years ago to make it possible for people like us to have a personal relationship with God today," our dad told us soberly. "We need to honor and respect that kind of sacrifice." Suddenly, those T-shirts in the gift shop didn't seem all that appealing. Those men came face-to-face with fear as we have never known and collided with it head-on. Centuries later their collision is still encouraging and leading people to faith. The wooden doors of the nearby college still bear scorch marks from those flames, physical reminders of their courage. Indeed, they did light a candle that day, and it has continued shining light into the dark corners of the earth hundreds of years later.

## COLLIDER BIO: D. L. MOODY

D. L. Moody is one of the most famous preachers of all time. It is estimated that over one million souls were saved directly through his ministry! However, Moody's influence did not only come from the pulpit. He made a commitment to talk to at least one person every day about Jesus, and he stayed true to this pledge.

Moody realized late one night that he had not shared his faith that day so he walked down the street and approached the first man he saw. The man rudely rejected Moody, storming off into the night. Moody returned home discouraged. It turned out the man knew who he was and badmouthed him about town.

Several weeks later Moody was climbing into bed when he heard a knock on his door. Moody cautiously opened his door and there stood that stranger, tears running down his face. He said, "Mr. Moody, I have not had a good night's sleep since that night you spoke to me under the lamp-post, and I have come around at this unearthly hour of the night for you to tell me what I have to do to be saved!"

Moody was determined to do faithfully what God asked of him, and God used him to change thousands of lives, both from the pulpit and one simple conversation at a time.

### "But You Jumped on One"

We opened this chapter with Carrie bungee jumping in New Zealand. After her jump, Carrie walked back up to the top of the hillside to join our dad. Dad was extremely proud of her and full of congratulations. But amid the praise, Carrie suddenly grew serious.

"Dad," she said, "I was afraid." Now that it was all over, Carrie was embarrassed at how fearful she was right before she jumped. To that our dad simply responded, "Carrie, courage is not the absence of fear. Courage is being scared to death and *still* jumping when the jump master says 'one.'" The jumping director told Carrie the longer she stood at the edge looking down, the harder it would be to jump. She would count down, three . . . two . . . one . . . , and on "one" Carrie was to go for it. Carrie stood in place at the edge of that tower, shaking like a leaf in a hurricane, but when the instructor got to "one," our brave little sis leapt off the edge, right on cue. She demonstrated enormous courage that day and humbled her brothers in the process.

Let's face it, being a Collider can be terrifying. But that's OK. Hey, at least it isn't *boring* to follow God. Rather, it's an incredible adventure. Unfortunately, some people know God wants them to take leaps of faith, but they stand right at the edge, frozen by fear. God is counting down, "three . . . two . . . one and a half . . . one and a quarter . . ." But they still stand there, hoping if they wait long enough, their fear will eventually subside and they'll be ready to take the plunge. They say, "I'll just wait where I am until I am comfortable doing this and *then* look out!" But long after the bungee instructor has turned off the lights, locked the doors, and gone home, those people are still standing at the edge of that tower muttering to themselves, "No, I'm still scared. Maybe in another hour, or day, or week, or year, or lifetime." Some people spend most of their lives standing one step away from experiencing all God has for them, but they can't bring themselves to take that important step.

## Fuel to the Fire

So what scares you? Is it the future? Rejection? Failing? Are you afraid God won't be there for you? Afraid you don't have what it takes? Hall of Fame NHL defenseman Ray Bourque knew his goaltender Patrick Roy was badly discouraged and beating himself up over a losing streak, so Bourque wisely encouraged him to "play for the joys of winning, not the fear of losing." Life is too brief to live it in fear. Rather, we must invest our energy for the joy of living. Doing things God's way may be frightening, challenging and at times confusing, but it will not be boring. Just remember, God isn't asking you to charge out into life and to do the best *you* can. That wouldn't necessarily amount to much. He is asking you to live your life in such a way you do the best *He* can as He lives His life *through* you.

We used to have a gas fire pit in our backyard. To light it you had to turn the gas on and then drop a match through the grate on top. The only problem was the match usually went out before it reached the gas on the bottom. So we'd have to get down dangerously close to the pit in order to shield the flame and then drop the match to ignite the gas. Mike figured this out the hard way. He cranked open the gas valve and vainly tried match after match with no success. When the fire finally ignited, a mushroom cloud of epic proportions burst out of the pit, nearly blowing him into the next neighborhood! Once Mike's eyebrows grew back, he was left with a powerful lesson. One match is pretty insignificant on its own. It flares up for a few fleeting seconds and produces little heat or light before it fizzles away. However, as soon as the match's small flame comes in contact with the powerful fuel, it erupts into a beautiful, bright flame that continues to burn long after the little match is snuffed out.

We are like matches on this earth. We flicker for a few brief moments and then quietly fade away. If we spend all our time worrying about what people will think of our tiny flame or if we're self-conscious that the meager heat we produce won't make a difference in our world, then our flame will go out, and it will be just as we feared. The reality is we don't have much to offer anyone apart from God.

However, when we draw close to Him and ask Him to be our source of fuel, that's when the fire burns. Alone we have every reason to be scared. Without Him we have every reason to doubt and to steer clear of collisions. But with God *all* things are possible (Luke 1:37). Jesus said, "But you will receive power when the Holy Spirit has come upon you, and you will be My witnesses in Jerusalem, in all Judea and Samaria, and to the ends of the earth" (Acts 1:8). God makes all the difference! Chances are, you fall in the "ends of the earth" category for the disciples at the time, but those of us in North America (a long way from Jerusalem) have faith because a handful of disciples were faithful to live by God's power. God is *your* power source. You may think you can't stand up to your friends and do the right thing or you can't get in front of people and share your testimony or you can't do whatever you know God is calling you to do. But you can!

How long have you stood peering over the edge of the platform, afraid to jump? Trust us. Waiting until tomorrow doesn't make it any easier. Have you been hiding away in a safe place, afraid to collide? Or have you been trying to blend in because you're afraid of what people might think if they find out you're a Christian? *Now* is the time to jump off the edge. *Now* is the time to let God take you through your fears. God wants to ignite your life into something brilliant. Don't be afraid of your worlds colliding, for the God who is with you is stronger than any force or person or problem you will ever collide with. Let today be the day you allow God to take you past your fears. Hold on because you're in for an amazing journey.

## SO WHAT?

1. Do you fear the unknown? What about your future most concerns you? What does your fear indicate about your view of God?

2. Do you fear rejection? What is the evidence that you do or do not? If you do, how does that reflect on your understanding

of God's love for you and His call on your life? How does it make you act around other people?

3. Do you fear failure? What is the evidence that you do or do not? If you do, what does that reveal about your belief in God's care for you? What effect does fear have on the way you live your life?

## WHAT NOW?

1. Why don't you try doing something that scares you to death and see how it isn't as bad as you always feared? Perhaps bungee jumping? Riding a roller coaster or a zip line? Maybe tell your youth pastor you'd like to share your testimony to the group or volunteer at your church somewhere scary (like child care).

2. Perhaps you can meet with some friends and share what fears you have that prevent you from serving God as you should. Then make a pact to help one another over the next three months to overcome those fears and to do what God is calling you to do.

3. Go to the back of your Bible and look up *fear* in the concordance. Read all the passages listed under this topic. Reflect on how these verses apply to your life. Are you living by these truths? If not, what is holding you back? Apply God's truth to specific instances you face during a typical week and remember them as you encounter each circumstance.

**Part 3**

# COLLIDING WITH YOUR PAIN

## Chapter 7

# WHEN THE COLLISION HURTS

*God whispers to us in our pleasures, speaks in our conscience, but shouts in our pains: it is His megaphone to rouse a deaf world.*[18]

—C. S. Lewis (Christian apologist and author)

*If God exists, either He can do nothing to stop the most egregious calamities, or He does not care to.*[19]

—Sam Harris (atheist Author)

### The Man, the Myth, the Delusional Cousin

Our cousin JP is an outrageous character, to put it mildly. The three of us grew up together in the same small town. One evening we were peacefully watching hockey in his basement when, without warning, we were ushered into "the Chi (pronounced *Chee*) Dynasty." Kicking open the basement door, JP cartwheeled into the room, his white childhood Tae Kwon Do belt fastened around his forehead. Scissor-kicking his way onto the coffee table, he confidently proclaimed, "I am Chi! And I feel *no* pain!"

Launching into a lightning fury of attacks, JP, or rather "Chi," turned the TV room into a battleground befitting Super Smash Bros. Despite his masterful command of the Crane fighting style, by sheer power of numbers, we soon overpowered the self-proclaimed Kung-Fu master. Each holding an arm, we ruthlessly targeted every pressure point we knew (and experimented with some new ones). Despite our assault, JP's gasping taunts still rang out, "You cannot hurt me! For I am Chi . . . and I feel . . . *no* pain!"

> ### CULTURE CLIP: *LOST*
>
> In 2004, the groundbreaking TV show *Lost* debuted and captured the hearts of millions of fans worldwide. It boasted all the elements of a good story: action, romance, humor, suspense, and an intricate plotline. However, it was the multilayered characters that kept fans watching.
>
> The show centered on the survivors of *Oceanic* Flight 815, a plane that crashed on a mysterious island. Each episode presented flashbacks of a particular character and the life they lived prior to the crash. As their stories (both past and present) unfolded, the viewers could see each character brought along much more "baggage" than what they checked plane-side.
>
> They were all shaped by significant hurts, disappointments, and losses from their past.
>
> Although the passengers were presented with a fresh start among the other strangers of the plane, they would each have to come to terms with the pain and failures of their past lives.

## Life Is Pain, Highness!

Eventually even the mighty fortress that was JP crumbled, and he was forced to accept a humbling reality: no one is immune to pain. In the movie *The Princess Bride*, Wesley exclaims to the heartbroken Princess Buttercup, "Life *is* pain, Highness! Anyone who says differently is selling something." *Preach it, Wes!* Pain is real, and each of us experiences it on a regular basis. Now we can strive to avoid pain as diligently as we should avoid 7-11's seventy-five-cent, one-minute, microwaveable, beef-and-cheese burritos (those should not be touched with a 39½ foot pole). However, regardless of the barriers we raise and our outward bravado, at some point we will inevitably go toe-to-toe with pain.

What kinds of hurt have you experienced? It's virtually impossible to survive childhood without regular episodes of physical bumps and bruises; they go along with exploring your world and learning to walk, to ride a bike, etc. If you are an athlete, you know all about aches and pain—sprains, torn ligaments, and possibly broken bones.

There are also emotional wounds. We've both experienced the misery of being targeted by bullies with all the accompanying barbs and threats. Perhaps you have a physical feature you've always hated, and it's like a slap in the face whenever someone teases you about it. A tragically high percentage of kids feel bewildered and helpless as they watch their parents drift further apart and talk of divorce. Have you ever gone through the misery of watching your longtime crush fall for someone else? Some pain will stay with us for the rest of our

> *Our effectiveness for God's kingdom rests largely upon how we collide with our pain.*

lives, from the day a loved one is ripped away instantaneously by a drunk driver or claimed by cancer. The list could go on indefinitely, but the point is we are *all* dealing with some form of affliction in our lives.

Collisions with painful life events are potentially devastating, physically, emotionally, and especially spiritually. The age-old question, How could a loving God allow bad things to happen? has no doubt pushed more people into unbelief than any other spiritual issue. Pain is the collision that spawns other dangerous parasites such as fear, doubt, bitterness, anger, and depression. So how do we navigate through a life that involves pain and suffering? Can we simply ignore it? When suffering invades our world and inflicts its battle wounds, will the casualties include a broken spirit? The million-dollar question is, Will we let our heartache drive our agenda, or will we stand firm in God's strength, responding the way He wants us to? It *is* possible

to come out of a collision not only intact, but stronger. The choices
we make when we are hurting carry repercussions not only for us but
also for those around us. Our effectiveness for God's kingdom rests
largely on how we collide with our pain.

## Lonely Hearts Club

Several years ago I (Mike) found myself in a sort of no-man's-
zone socially. Most of my best buddies moved away for college or
work, whereas I was cutting costs by living at home. Those who
remained in our college group began dating others in the group, and
I often felt like a third wheel. I was a leader in our college ministry but
was losing the desire to participate. I went through the motions and
did what was expected of me but only out of duty.

Finally I decided to take my frustrations and hurts to a friend of
mine, Al, who was the director of our college ministry. We went for
lunch, and I poured out my miseries to him. I told him I was lonely
and tired of being a leader. No one seemed to appreciate my hard
work. Everyone just wanted what I could give, but no one ever gave
back. I dumped months of bitterness onto the table. Why did nobody
notice or care how miserable *I* was?

Al patiently listened to my tirade until I wore myself out. I figured
he'd have no patience for the way our college group was acting, and
he'd tell me how to whip them into shape. Instead he hit me between
the eyes.

"Do you remember what Keith shared with us last night?" he
asked me.

I had to stop and think and could vaguely recall that Keith,
a newcomer to our group, spoke about his home situation. "Oh yeah,"
I replied, "Keith is going through some stuff at home."

"Not just *stuff*," corrected Al. He went on to recap Keith's
story, during which I had evidently been daydreaming: Keith's
parents abandoned him. One was in prison; both were in bondage
to substance abuse. Keith was left alone to support himself and his
younger sister. Al's piercing gaze met mine, and he asked, "What did

you say to him after he shared last night?" My heart sank. I hadn't said anything to him. In fact, I was in such a hurry to leave I bolted as soon as I could. Now that it was Al's turn to speak, he was turning the tables on me. He gently but pointedly reminded me of the painful circumstances several of the young adults in our church were going through—big stuff. One was losing her mom to cancer; another had Hodgkin's disease; another was diagnosed with a mental illness. I was too preoccupied with my own misery to see the pain all around me. That day Al held up a mirror to me so I could see my disillusionment for the pity party it really was. I was caving in under my personal discouragement, and Al was telling me to get out there and collide.

## Caving In to Pain

We are never more selfish than when we are hurting. There is for sure a time and place for grieving, and we'll talk about that later; but God commands us to love others *all* the time, not just when our own lives are peachy. If we're called to show love only when we feel warm and fuzzy, then Jesus did not understand love since He loved His enemies even as they pounded nails into His hands. When life doesn't play out the way we want it to, we can respond by drawing nearer to God and reaching out to others, or we can become a hollow ghost, dragging our burdens around like the chains of Jacob Marley in *A Christmas Carol,* growing frustrated when no one seems to care or understand. The choice is completely ours—focus inward

> We are never more selfish than when we are hurting.

and play the suffering saint or do as Jesus did and turn our attention outward to the hurting people around us.

When we cave in to our pain and obsess over how it affects us, there are a couple of potentially damaging responses. One is when we lash out in fury at whatever or whomever it is we blame for our suffering. A friend of ours once broke off a relationship because her boyfriend was acting increasingly more manipulative. Almost immediately she started getting hate mail from his parents. They once loved her and dearly wanted their son to marry her. But now they were assailing her with ridiculous accusations and assigning evil motives to her actions. What caused them to act like that? They were acting out of deep pain. Our uncle has a saying: "Hurt people hurt people." And that, sadly, is true.

A second unhealthy outcome of caving in is isolation. We want to be all alone so we can tend our wounds in peace and privacy. Pain can separate good friends, divide families, and pull Christians out of their church just when they need spiritual encouragement the most. We grow irritated and frustrated when no one realizes all the burdens we bear, so we slowly distance ourselves from our parents, our friends, and our church. Like a turtle we draw in to our shell where nothing can touch us. We justify our withdrawal, saying, "Nobody understands me." Isolation is an instinctive response to pain. When God appears unwilling to offer immediate answers to our cries for help, our relationship with Him can likewise fall victim to our inward retreat.

But isolation doesn't help. We were not created to live selfishly, so selfish living will never make us happy. The world offers various self-centered solutions to

---

**CULTURE CLIP: IRON MAN**

Tony Stark is a wealthy playboy who is content simply to live for life's pleasures. He has everything he wants and does not care about anyone else. This all changes when he is captured by terrorists.

While testing a new weapon in the Middle East, Tony is captured by evil men and forced to build a powerful missile, but he deceives them and instead creates the first version of the iconic Iron Man suit in order to escape.

A fellow prisoner named Wellington Yinsen helps Tony design the suit and ultimately sacrifices his life to buy Tony the time he needs to complete it. As Tony cradles the head of his dying friend, Yinsen gives the former pleasure seeker this simple advice: "Don't waste your life."

From that moment on, the superhero Iron Man is born and devotes his life to saving and protecting others. It took Tony's most painful moments to teach him a life lived for selfish gain ultimately has no purpose.

pain and numerous inspirational quotes about picking oneself up off the ground and jumping back in the game. Christians aren't driven by self-sufficiency, yet we often try to deal with our hurt the same way the world does. Recently a friend of ours was going through a tough time, so he tried to ease the pain by buying a case of beer and holing up in his basement to watch movies. But he woke up the next morning to realize he only succeeded in adding physical discomfort to his emotional pain. How pathetic is it

> We were not created to live selfishly, so selfish living will never make us happy.

to try drinking away our hurt in a dark, lonely basement? That's what caving in to pain looks like when we follow the world's example and put all the focus on us.

## My Teeth: A Tragic Tale in Seven Acts

Recently I (Dan) received notice from my dentist that I was past due for my annual checkup. Reluctantly, my younger sister Carrie and I booked appointments. We've had different track records with our teeth. Carrie has never experienced a cavity while I got about a one per appointment ratio going. But this time I was determined things would be different.

Sure enough Carrie, dentist's pet, kept her perfect record intact. The dentist called me next, but this time I was ready.

I knew full well I thought about flossing the same number of times I thought about long-haired Tibetan mountain goats (OK, maybe even less), that my current toothbrush's life span dated back to the Victorian era, and that every time I smiled into a mirror I half expected to see Dorothy and Toto skipping along, singing "Follow the yellow brick road." So I bought a high quality tooth bleach kit. *Poof!* My teeth were white as snow. My dentist would never know the difference.

Confident in my scheme, I cheerfully popped into the chair and flashed a dazzling smile. After all the usual torture was performed, my dentist returned holding my X-rays. He looked stunned. *Ha! Didn't expect these perfect chompers, did you!*

Taking a deep breath, he began: "Mr. Blackaby, you have three cavities"—*three! In one appointment! Wow, I never thought*—"on your bottom jaw. There's another four on the upper. Now, allow me to demonstrate some helpful brushing techniques."

It took three full appointments to complete my fillings. Carrie remarked on the drive home that they could construct a smart car with the amount of tin they'd be cramming into my mouth. *Oh snap!*

## Pain as a Cave Dweller

Avoiding life's problems won't make them disappear; usually avoidance makes things worse. Boys can't show emotion, and big girls don't cry, right? At least that's what the world tells us. So men let their families fall apart because they're too prideful to admit anything is wrong. Women bottle up their hurt until it explodes, their angry words leaving friends and family scarred and bewildered. Refusing to acknowledge pain does not make it go away.

You've probably heard that ostriches bury their heads in the sand to avoid danger, and you've no doubt concluded "ostriches are idiots." Well, they may not be the sharpest bird in the species, but in their defense ostriches actually aren't acting kamikaze and suffocating themselves. They are in fact attempting to look like a bush. They lay their long neck and head on the ground so the only thing a predator sees is their big feathery body, which it hopefully mistakes for some shrubbery. Either way the ostrich is doing whatever a big bird has to do not to get eaten.

We're a bit higher up on the food chain, but humans do our best to avoid pain too. Cave Dwellers seek refuge from pain within the walls of their comfortable church life. They veil their problems and fears in a masquerade of spirituality. When pain eventually seeps into their cave, they petition God to make their cave more cozy. What are the most routine prayer requests? "God, please give me healing." "Help me pass this exam!" "Give us sunny weather." "Take away this stress," and so on. The common denominator is an emphasis on what *we* want. If you keep a prayer journal, take a quick perusal through the last year to see what consumed your prayer life, including the petitions you offered up for others. Is there a thread of "make life more comfy" weaving through your entries? How much effort do we expend asking God what might be on *His* heart? How many times have we said "amen" to close off a lengthy "gimme list" and gotten on with our day, never considering what God might have to say to us, or that it might make us uncomfortable?

One summer vacation we joined another family to spend a few days at the beach. After splashing around in the warm water for awhile and constructing

> *Cave Dwellers don't just miss out on serving Christ; ironically, they also miss the amazing life that He promised.*

the mother of all sand castles, we kids returned to home base, where the lawn chairs, snacks, and umbrellas were stationed. Sitting in two nicely shaded chairs were our mom and our friends' dad. They hadn't budged since we arrived. We asked them why they hadn't left their beach bunker. Didn't they enjoy the beach? Mom responded, "Oh, I *love* the beach—except for the water—too many icky parasites!" "Uncle Lou" (as we called him) chimed in, "And *I* love the beach too if it weren't for all the sand!" They would eventually depart the beach perfectly dry and sand-free, accompanied by our dad, who also "loves the beach" except for the hot sun.

That's the problem with the avoidance tactic; you miss out on so many things while trying to stay safe and comfortable. Cave Dwellers have a hard time living for Jesus. Our physical eyes can only point one direction at a time (unless you're our sister, but that's just freaky). It's the same with our spiritual eyes. If they're focused inward, they can't look outward toward God or other people. Cave Dwellers don't just miss out on serving Christ; ironically they also miss the amazing life He promised. As kids (and later as adults who still *act* like kids), we loved bumper cars. Did you ever notice there's always at least one kid who avoids the chaos and carnage by taking a joyride around the perimeter? When the power finally shuts down, the nonparticipant has successfully avoided getting bumped but has also missed most of the fun. If we want to impact our friends and family with the love of God they so desperately need, then we must expect some collisions along the way.

> *If we ask God to make us more like Jesus, then we shouldn't be surprised when He introduces a cross into our lives.*

So, if Cave-Ins explode (or implode) at the first sign of conflict and Cave Dwellers try to avoid collisions altogether, what do Colliders do?

## Colliding with Our Pain

Have you ever been told that to discover God's will for your life you should simply look at what passions He gave you and do what you love doing? While we should definitely use our talents to serve God, is it safe to assume God's purpose for us will always involve what we enjoy and what consistently lines up with our preferences? Undoubtedly, being brutally beaten and murdered on a cross weren't high on Jesus' Things I Enjoy list. In fact, His prayer was, "Father, if You are willing, take this cup away from Me—*nevertheless*, not My will, but Yours, be done" (Luke 22:42). It follows then, that if we want to live like Jesus, we may walk some pretty difficult paths.

How often do we pray or sing worship songs asking God to make us more like Jesus? Then why are we so shocked when He introduces a cross into our lives? Jesus suffered undeservedly by being tortured, beaten, lied to, lied about, and abandoned. When He asked His closest friends to stay up just one night and pray for Him, they couldn't even do that. Jesus was just hours away from capture and brutal execution, but His core group slept like babies. They didn't know the full scope of what the next horrific hours would bring their Teacher, but surely they could see in His demeanor that He had a heavy heart and hear in His voice that He needed them. Yet, even though they let Him down, Jesus loved them, forgave them, and ultimately died for them. If we truly want to be like Christ, we are to think of other people, even in our most agonizing times. We are to forgive not only those who caused our pain but also those who betrayed us or stood by and did nothing to help in our time of need. *That's* colliding with pain.

## A Time to Mourn

So, if we're not to focus on ourselves when we're hurting and we're supposed to look outward because others experience pain too, does that mean pain doesn't hurt? Of course not. Pain hurts a lot. Life can deal out some rotten hands. Dan's wife Sarah lost her dad in a snow avalanche when she was five years old. When she walked down the aisle to become Dan's bride, she didn't have her dad with her; instead she placed a rose on an empty chair in his honor. That's pain and it hurts. Many Christians think it's unspiritual to grieve or to weep. "God is good all the time, and all the time God is good!" they proclaim, trying to put on a cheerful face when inside they are screaming out to God, "Why did You let this happen?" If this has been you, you have the freedom to exhale. The Bible says there *is* "a time to weep and a time to laugh, a time to mourn and a time to dance" (Eccl. 3:4). In fact, a common theme in the book of Psalms is called "lament," which is basically a pouring out of grief to God. Many of David's psalms could have been plucked straight from the diary of a high school student, verbalizing deep hurt and confusion. What's important to note is that though he experienced bereavement and sorrow, David never lost his trust in God.

The problem is not that we feel pain; the problem is when we dwell there long after the time for grieving is past. The world has no hope apart from their present experience. But Christians know the God of the universe can carry them through life's darkest valleys and give them hope and peace in spite of the circumstances. After a painful breakup, once you've wrecked a jumbo-sized tub of cookie-dough ice cream and cried your tears, if you let that event tie a knot in your self-esteem and define you as a bitter person, then pain has claimed another victory. To be a Collider does not mean you are invincible;

it's a commission to stay focused on Jesus in the midst of your ordeal. Draw near to God, and He will draw near to you (James 4:8).

## Your Friendly Neighborhood Insomniac, Part 1 (Dan's Story)

My early teenage years weren't easy. I (Dan) always lagged a few fashion trends behind the pack, and with my un-styled shoulder-length hair and full set of braces (accompanied by the ever-present pool of drool bubbling out the side of my mouth), I would never be mistaken for one of the "cool kids." Then, during this awful period, another problem developed: I stopped sleeping.

I was experiencing several other changes at the time. My voice transformed from Mickey Mouse to James Earl Jones, and "Cooties Clara" was making my heart beat faster. I trusted my newfound sleep dilemma would stabilize with the other changes. It didn't. Actually it got worse.

*To be a Collider does not mean you must be invincible; it is a commission to stay focused on Jesus in the midst of your ordeal.*

As months passed and my sleep continued to deteriorate, I began desperately searching for a solution. Daily exercise was one option, but I decided that was a more painful burden than not sleeping. So I tried various diets and routines (a real man can appreciate a good ol' bubble bath from time to time) and was single-handedly keeping the sleeping-pill industry booming.

But my insomnia stretched over the next year. It reached the point where a *good* night was falling asleep before 6:00 a.m., and it was not uncommon to endure as many as three complete days without any rest. Staggering around the house like a zombie, I struggled to function. My academics (which were already nothing to write home about) sunk to even lower depths, and I was constantly on edge. However, the worst part wasn't the exhaustion but the loneliness. I'd say good-night to my family and then descend into the basement to spend the next six or seven hours alone. It became unbearable.

I finally checked into a professional sleep clinic where psychologists and doctors specialized in sleep disorders. After various tests the chief doctor returned. I was ecstatic! I was finally going to have my answers.

Without even bothering to open my file, he simply looked me in the eye and confessed, "Daniel, we're sorry. Unfortunately we cannot determine a cause for your insomnia. We can't help you." I collapsed back into my seat, winded. *Why?* I asked myself. I couldn't understand why God continued to let me be disappointed.

During this time I was heavily involved on my church worship team, as well as in a leadership role within my youth group. I volunteered on all the youth mission trips and to my knowledge did everything God told me to do. So *why* did God still let me suffer? If anything, I thought, my misery was *hindering* me from being an effective Christian. I prayed fervently, yet God left this burden in my life.

Have you ever found yourself in that place? Lonely? Confused? Frustrated? Mad at God? One of the greatest lies in existence (alongside McDonalds' "healthy" menu) is that God does not intend for His people to suffer. That simply isn't true.

There is no bleaker feeling than being informed you can't be helped (if I had a dime for every time a biology tutor told me that). I was young and apparently healthy but exhausted to the brink of insanity so it was inevitable that I would eventually break down, and I did.

The house was dead quiet, and I sat unmoving on the basement floor, feeling unbearably lonely. Glancing at my clock, I saw it was 3:00 a.m. A gut feeling told me it would be another all-nighter. I just couldn't take it anymore.

I cried out to God, "Why are You letting me go through this? Don't You love me? I've been praying for two years; haven't You heard me? Can't you see how much this is affecting my life? God, if You *do* love me, I need You to reveal it to me because I just can't see You right now." My gut was right; I spent the rest of the night awake and miserable.

A few days later something peculiar happened: I received a letter. This was odd for three reasons: (1) it implied I was popular enough to get a letter, (2) in a generation of Facebook and text messaging, this antiquated form of communication was almost medieval. I wasn't even sure what to click on to make it open. And (3) the letter was from my friend Kelley who lived a mere stone's throw from my house. I curiously tore open the envelope and pulled out a bright pink piece of paper. On it was written:

> *Daniel,*
>
> *I just wanted to write you a note to see how you're doing. I've been praying for you lots lately. God's really laid you on my heart lately, and I don't know why yet, but I felt like I need to continue to pray for and encourage you. God works in mysterious ways, so maybe me being inspired to write you a note is part of a bigger picture I can't see.*
>
> *In His Service*
>
> *Kelley*
>
> *(ps. Sorry the paper's pink)*
>
> *Matthew 11:28–30*

What an answer to prayer! Full of emotion I sprinted to her house. Asking her about the note, I discovered she wrote it the same night I called out to God in my basement. She said, "It was funny. I came home from a volleyball tournament, totally exhausted, flopped on my bed, and was instantly asleep. But I woke up in the night and couldn't get you off my mind. I'd never done anything like this before, but I just felt I had to write you that note."

"Out of curiosity," I asked, a chill running down my spine, "do you remember what time you got up to write it?"

She thought for a second and then nodded, "Yeah, I remember, it was 3:00 a.m."

In that moment God revealed Himself to me as He never had before. His love was so evident I felt as if I could physically feel it wrapping around me. Even while I was praying, God was waking Kelley to answer my prayer. If we never experienced darkness, we'll never appreciate light. The darker the world around us, the more brilliant the light of Jesus appears. However, it requires us to hold out through the night.

### Eye of the Storm

As with Dan's sleep struggles, pain presents us the opportunity to draw closer to God. Often in our hardest times we turn to the One we so often neglect in happier days. The great British author Charles Dickens wrote in his novel *Great Expectations*, "Suffering has been stronger than all other teaching. . . . I have been bent and broken, but—I hope—into a better shape."[20] Through our pain we can allow God to mold us so we look more like Jesus. This attitude collides head-on with a world that tells you, "Life is short. Seek pleasure at all costs and flee from pain." When pain threatens to overwhelm you, cling to Jesus. Not only will He help you ride out

### COLLIDER TESTIMONY: SARAH SUTHERLAND—TWENTY YEARS OLD

When I was a five-year-old, I said good-bye to my father at the base of a mountain for his day of snowmobiling, I had no idea it would be last time I would ever see him. One avalanche later my life was changed forever.

Growing up without a father was really hard. I spent several years in counseling because the mention of him would bring me to tears. As I grew older, I began dealing with the pain by pushing it deep inside.

In tenth grade things began to boil over. I struggled to keep my pain hidden. When a classmate realized I was having a hard time, he invited me to his church the following Sunday. I was not a church-goer, but I accepted. When we got there, we realized it was Father's Day Sunday. The pastor preached how God is the Father to the fatherless, and the sermon couldn't have been more perfect. That day God began to heal my broken and burdened heart, and He's never let me go.

Shortly after, I went on my first mission trip to Africa. I didn't really understand how God could use me there, but as we attended some orphanages, I felt a strong connection to the children. Like me, they suffered the loss of family members and were dealing with that pain. I shared my story with them, and I know God used me to touch them in a way no other team member could. They got to hear of how the same God who comforted me was now reaching out to heal their broken hearts.

the storm, but He will use it to make you stronger for the next collision that inevitably comes.

We shamelessly enjoy disaster flicks. The plots are usually atrocious, and the acting better suits a third-grade drama class. But there is something appealing about watching total destruction in all its CGI glory. One particular favorite is the 2004 film *The Day After Tomorrow*. In the plot, an immense storm passes over America. The heroes manage to evade death by holing up in a library and avoiding the outside subzero temperatures. At a crucial point the characters realize that the winds have died down. They have entered the eye of the storm (cue the music).

How do they respond? By sitting back and relaxing in the calmness? No, they dash out from cover and feverishly gather as many supplies as they can carry. Why? Because the eye of the storm will soon pass, and they will be tossed back out into the violent hurricane, so they get ready for the collision. They prepare themselves because they realize many out in the storm need rescuing.

When God allows us moments of peace and recharging, we shouldn't assume life's storms are over. The apostle Paul was no stranger to hardship. His list (see 1 Cor. 11) included being imprisoned, beaten, whipped, stoned, shipwrecked, and an array of other physical suffering (and we complain about slow Internet). In addition he sustained the mental and emotional wounds inflicted by those who hated him along with betrayal and rejection by some of his alleged friends. And he had his famous, mysterious "thorn in the flesh." Considering how much this apostle suffered on Christ's behalf, you'd think God would grant him some comfort. If anyone deserved a break, Paul did. Yet the Father's response was, "My grace is sufficient for you" (2 Cor. 12:9). God doesn't promise to remove our every ache

> *We are not necessarily doubting that God will do the best for us; we are wondering how painful the best will turn out to be.*
> —C. S. Lewis

and pain; however, He *does* pledge never to leave or forsake us (Josh. 1:5).

We want God to give us a painfree life and to make us happy, but instead He offers us joy in *any* circumstance. While the world looks to better cars, faster computers, more money, prettier girlfriends, more understanding boyfriends, bigger thrills, and taller drinks to make them forget about their pain and squeeze some joy out of life, Christians cling to Jesus. He's the only One who offers *true* joy, the kind nothing can take away (John 16:22). That's why Paul and Silas could sing praises to God after they were brutally beaten and thrown into prison (Acts 16:25). Do you want a happiness that can be snatched away by the slightest shift in life's winds or a joy that stands firm against even the fiercest gales? Do you know Jesus in this way? Perhaps your relationship with God has been sidelined by other

---

## COLLIDER BIO: HORATIO G. SPAFFORD

Horatio G. Spafford was a highly esteemed Chicago-based attorney during the 1800s. Spafford decided to take his wife and four daughters to England to accompany his friend, the great evangelist D. L. Moody, on his tour. Due to pressing business, he sent his family on ahead, planning to join them later. Sailing aboard the SS *Ville du Havre*, his family and 306 fellow passengers embarked on the long voyage to England.

On November 22, disaster struck when their ship was accidentally hit by an English vessel. Chaos erupted on deck as passengers frantically attempted to launch the lifeboats. There wasn't time. In a mere twelve minutes the vessel was sunk. Along with the ship, 226 passengers perished that night, including all four of Spafford's daughters.

Boarding the next available ship, a brokenhearted Spafford departed slowly across the Atlantic to join his wife. When the ship's captain informed him they were currently sailing over the spot where the SS *Ville du Havre* sank, Spafford began penning the words to a song. We know it today as the classic hymn "It Is Well With My Soul." The opening stanza goes like this:

*When peace, like a river, attendeth my way, when sorrows like sea billows roll; whatever my lot, thou hast taught me to say, It is well, it is well with my soul.*

things. But when the storms come, only one relationship can stand firm even if everything else crumbles around you. Have you invested in that relationship? Don't wait until your life begins falling apart to pray. The best way to deal with storms is to have a firm foundation before they ever hit. Hard times are coming. They are inevitable. Are you ready?

## Your Friendly Neighborhood Insomniac, Part 2

In a storybook finale to my story, I (Dan) probably would have been dramatically healed upon touching the pink note and slept like Rip Van Winkle. But thankfully life isn't scripted by Disney because God had much bigger plans. My insomnia remained even after Kelley's note. We aren't always called to understand, but we are called to have faith, and I had a renewed hope that God heard my prayer.

At summer youth camp a few months later, God finally revealed the whole story. The camp involves several churches, and the campers mix together for activities all week. But traditionally our church group would meet one evening to share what God was doing among us. To be honest I was never fond of those times. It always became a circus with a few specific girls emptying their tear ducts and apologizing to one another for the same old petty things as they had the previous four summers.

This particular night, however, the emotional dam had not yet broken so I got the ball rolling, "I know I'm a broken record. My insomnia is still bad. Keep praying, maybe God will finally take it away."

"I need to share," came a soft voice from across the room. It was a sixteen-year-old girl who attended our youth group. "This has been the hardest year of my life. Between a sticky family situation, an unhealthy dating relationship, and hanging with the wrong crowd, I drifted from God. I came home really late from a party one night, slightly drunk, and feeling miserable. I seriously considered taking my life. I logged-in to chat online and noticed Daniel was the only one still on. We weren't close, but I needed to vent. I started unloading all my anger, but slowly our conversation shifted back to my faith.

Though it was almost 5:00 a.m., we met in person to talk, and by the end of that night, I rededicated my life to God. If Daniel had not been awake, I would still be running from God—or dead."

She barely finished when a guy spoke up: "I've also had the worst year of my life. The situation at home hasn't been good, been into bad stuff. I couldn't take it. I strapped ice bags to my wrists and planned to slash them after they were numb, but I felt I needed to tell at least one person. It was 4:00 a.m., and I remembered Daniel would probably be awake. Sure enough he answered the phone right away, and we talked for the rest of the night. We met for breakfast the next morning, and here I am. I can say for sure that if Daniel had not been up that night, I would be dead."

Speechless, I watched a domino effect around the room. Four more teens said they reached their

## COLLIDER BIO: PAIGE ARMSTRONG

Paige Armstrong was a typical, carefree ten-year-old girl. Like most young girls, she liked to sing and dance. However, she also had something most ten-year-old girls didn't—cancer. What was assumed to be strong growing pains was ultimately revealed to be a rare cancerous tumor on her leg bone called Ewing's sarcoma.

For the next year Paige went through medical horrors no young girl should ever have to endure. But God never left her side. As she would later say, "My purpose came through pain." During this trying time in her life, God crossed her path with the Make-A-Wish Foundation who granted her wish of recording a CD.

Her inspirational victory over cancer led to interviews with major television networks. She began traveling across the nation sharing the hope she found. But God was just beginning. He opened the doors for Paige to host a weekly TV show as well as publish a book sharing her story. Her Make-A-Wish demo landed her a record deal and her debut CD entitled *Wake Up* was released shortly after. She shared with us, "I couldn't believe how God was using the trial He allowed in my life to impact others! All I could do was step aside and smile. He *knew* what He was doing all along." In a way only God can, He took Paige's horrific situation and used it to change lives across America.

"He's shown me that life is precious. It's a mist, and good gracious . . . we *can't* waste it!" —Paige Armstrong lowest points at a time when their pastors, parents, and friends were all asleep, but I was there to help them. In that humbling experience I realized, while I was so focused on my discomfort, I was completely missing the amazing wonders God wanted to perform through my life to help others.

*God doesn't waste pain.* Christians aren't joyful because they are immune to pain but rather because their perspective goes beyond the hurt. Even in the midst of personal tragedy, Christians can be used to impact eternity. Colliders look past distress and acknowledge what God can do through struggles. We may not choose what life throws our way, but we *do* decide what our response will be.

> *We may not choose what life throws our way, but we do decide what our response will be.*

We have to get over looking at life as unfair. When Dan sat in his quiet house while his family slept, he didn't understand why God allowed him to suffer that unique trial. But his personal story has allowed him to help others in a unique way too. Since that time, Dan has been able to share his story with audiences around North America as well as other continents. A large church recently filmed and interviewed him telling about his experience. That video has now been viewed by thousands of people, and several of them have written to say how it helped them collide with similar arduous circumstances. Writing his story in this book is yet another amazing way God is using his pain to encourage all kinds of people he'll never meet. Amazingly enough, although Dan didn't do anything differently, after that summer his sleep slowly began to improve. Today he no longer struggles with insomnia. God knew it was going to be an especially hard summer in our town, and He chose Dan to reach out to those teenagers at an hour when no one else could.

Michael was a man in our church who experienced the bewildering pain of life without a father. When other boys were playing catch with their dads in the front yard, he could only sit back and watch. No one would have judged him for being angry at God. Now, as a grown man, he initiated and helps run a unique ministry that reaches out to fatherless boys to spend time with them hiking, playing sports, and enjoying numerous activities. He works regular hours at a fast food place to pay the bills, but he does the ministry out of the overflow of his heart. Michael's painful growing-up experience has allowed him to connect and interact with these boys in a way many others could not. He knows what they are going through and so has a unique opportunity to give them hope.[21]

We spent some time in Athens, Greece, one summer doing refugee work. While there we met an amazing man; we'll just call him Steve. Steve was a Muslim from Iraq, who fled the country in the midst of the war, eventually landing in Athens. Living in a one-room, abandoned building with six other men and only possessing the clothing on his back, Steve had an encounter with God that changed his life. When we met Steve, we did not meet a bitter, cynical man. Instead he was one of the most joyous guys we'd ever been around (and a killer fooseball player). Despite his rough life, Steve realized God gave him a unique testimony and ability to impact the hopeless refugees around him in a way an ignorant group of privileged North Americans like us never could. He chose the right attitude, and God used him to bring joy to many people as a result. How about you? What's your story? It's easy to get discouraged the moment hardship digs in its fangs, but could it be that perhaps God is preparing to do an amazing work through your life that only *you* can do?

## Head-On Collision: A Different Kind of Response

Several years ago we got a phone call no one wants to receive. Our mother and little sister were in a serious car accident and were being rushed to the hospital. While driving on the highway at full speed, an oncoming van hit an ice patch, spun out of control, and collided head-on with our mother who was also driving full speed. As we raced to the hospital, we passed the scene of the collision. They closed off the highway so they could remove the carnage. A mangled, smoking, scrap of crumbled metal was faintly recognizable as our family minivan. Blood and glass covered the snowy ditch.

Reaching the hospital, we were brought to our sister's room. Small glass chips stuck out from her hair, and minor bruising covered most of her body but thankfully nothing more. Our mother had unfortunately not escaped as harm-free. Having heroically swerved the van, she took the brunt of the impact. Serious cuts and bruises covered her body, and her right kneecap was shattered. When we arrived, she was being taken away for surgery. She looked us in the eyes as she was wheeled away and confidently told us, "God looked out for us today." She was clinging to Jesus, worshipping Him even in her battered condition.

The police would later say their survival was nothing short of a miracle. But our mom, an adamant jogger who recently finished her first 10K, had run her last race. A continuous throbbing pain will remind her of the accident for the rest of her life, and she most likely will never experience another peaceful sleep due to the pain. Emergency workers used the Jaws of Life to pry the other driver from her crumpled vehicle, then airlifted her to the hospital. She too had multiple but not life-threatening injuries. But instead of being angry at the careless driver, Mom did something unexpected.

Buying a tiny fragile china plate from the hospital gift shop, she wrote on the back: "Life is fragile" and "God is good." She added a card with a short note explaining that she was a Christian and she believed God spared them both. She said she would be praying for the lady daily as they both recovered.

Mom later discovered the other driver was the longtime neighbor of a local pastor's wife, whose name is Kathy. Kathy called Mom to ask for prayer for her friend and was delighted to hear God had already used our mom to reach out to the woman, who was not a Christian.

## Summary

Painful circumstances are unavoidable collisions. We all have stories we could tell about the hardships we've faced. However, we probably have fewer stories of how God used us *in the midst* of our pain. We don't pretend to understand everything about pain. Ultimately only God knows why atrocities happen in this world. However, we *do* know God wants us to trust Him to bring us through it, and He can use our pain to show others His love.

Pain is a thief that can rob you from being used by God if you let it. All around you are others who need your help. Don't lose sight of that in the midst of the dark times. It's OK to feel grief, but that is only for a season. Don't let your pain make you selfish. Christians are not immune to the sting of life's trials, but Colliders hold fast to God, knowing their pain offers a unique opportunity to grow stronger and to minister to others who are hurting. Are you open to God using you in this way? We guarantee it will be a collision you never forget.

## SO WHAT?

1.  Jot down something that's causing you pain right now. Then think of a Scripture verse or promise from God that addresses your pain. Reflect on how you are handling your pain. Have you been like a Cave-In? A Cave Dweller? A Collider? What is the evidence?
2.  List three positive things God has done in your life as a result of the pain He has allowed you to go through.

## WHAT NOW?

1.  Take a half-day retreat. Make a list of those things causing you the most pain. Hold each one up to God in prayer and ask Him to give you peace, understanding, and comfort in the midst of your pain. Record what you learn.
2.  Think of at least one person presently experiencing pain. Reach out to them and seek to comfort and encourage him or her. You may pass on a blessing just when another person needs it most.

3. If you've been trying to act invincible to pain, find a Christian adult whom you respect and share what you're going through. May the Lord comfort you and give you His strength as you turn your hurting heart over to Him. And then may He use your life to bless others as well.

# Part 4

# COLLIDING WITH POP CULTURE

# Chapter 8

## RECOGNIZING THE COLLISION— SATAN'S POISON GAS

*Immersion in today's highly influential, mindless, soulless, spiritually delusional popular culture has resulted in our high literacy in popular culture and low literacy in our faith.*[22]

—Dick Staub (Christian author/pop culture scholar)

*The Beatles are more popular than Jesus.*

—John Lennon, 1966 (singer/songwriter of The Beatles)

### Attack!

It's everywhere. It's pervading presence is unavoidable. It is constantly bombarding us and relentlessly luring us into its ensnaring vise grip. It is popular culture (although if you guessed Starbucks you get half credit). Flashy billboards line the highways, and tabloid magazines dominate every checkout counter. Even Snickers bar wrappings are plastered with images of an upcoming summer blockbuster.

In the 1985 book *Amusing Ourselves to Death*, Neil Postman commented on the disastrous direction his nation was taking as Americans grew increasingly enamored with entertainment. He wrote, "Television is our culture's principle mode of knowing about itself. Therefore—and this is the critical point—how television stages the world becomes the model for how the world is properly to be staged."[23] In other words, the way we view the world is intricately connected to what we see on TV. The images on our screens carry messages about how the world *is* and how the world *should* be, what is *normal* and what is *moral*. Because of this, the entertainment business can be Satan's primary mouthpiece. We're bombarded daily with values and attitudes that completely contradict the life Christ modeled. What is really scary is how much pop culture permeates our society. It has seeped into every aspect of our daily lives. If Christians aren't careful, our lives will start to look more like the *The Simpsons* than like Jesus. Even churches have fallen under the spell of entertainment. Sunday services are organized to reflect *Late Night with David Letterman* rather than a worship offering to God. Many churches, fearful of losing their "audience" try to compete with Hollywood. Surely we *should* stay current, but to package the gospel into what we see on our HD surround sound home theater entertainment system with the assumption young people are incapable of taking in anything that isn't amusing does our generation a disservice. Young

## CULTURE CLIP: TIGER VS. TERRORISTS

When the world's most marketable athlete, Tiger Woods, was exposed for carrying on a secret extramarital life with multiple women, his shameful secrets saturated the news. Millions of Americans gobbled up the salacious details as his mistresses spewed out far too much information.

The scandal set a *New York Times* record by appearing on the front page for an amazing twenty consecutive days, breaking the previous record held by the 9/11 terrorist attacks, sadly revealing what Americans *really* want to read about.

adults don't need more diversion; we have plenty of that everywhere we turn. When the church tries to go head-to-head with Hollywood, it will lose. Hollywood has more resources and experience in entertainment. They are pros. But the church does not exist to entertain; it exists for something much deeper—to encounter and serve God.

## The Silent Killer

Our great grandfather G. R. S. Blackaby served in World War I. During his commission he stared straight into death's icy face numerous times. Thankfully, he kept a journal and recorded some of his hair-raising experiences. He wrote that the deadliest weapon he faced was not the artillery shells that constantly rained upon his unit or the stream of machine-gun bullets spewing toward his trench. It was an insidious silent killer—poisonous chemical gas. On several occasions he barely escaped with his life from those perilous gas raids. Many of his comrades were not so fortunate.

Pop culture is like that poisonous gas. Like a cruise missile it flies under the radar and overtakes us because we are oblivious to the danger in our midst. It is both flashy and subversive at the same time, and it's something we welcome into our lives too readily. After a long day of classes or work, we flip on the TV without really thinking about it. We're tired and drained, and we want something to distract us from our problems for a while. We jump on YouTube, power up our iPod, or watch a DVD to escape the hectic struggles of everyday life. We turn to pop culture when we *don't want* to collide. The problem is most everything we watch on TV reflects the perspective of its non-Christian creators. The entertainment industry pervades every aspect of our lives, and this constant barrage of godless thinking bombards us on a continual basis *every day*. How could it *not* influence the way we think, the way we act, the way we make choices, the way we live?

Surely Satan's deadliest weapon to derail our generation from following God is entertainment, not because entertainment itself is bad but because it comes to us in our unguarded moments as we veg, transfixed in front of a screen, leaving all inhibitions and filters behind. God help us if we model our lives after *The Bachelor* instead of the Bible. So what are Christians supposed to do in a world saturated with anti-Christian media? Well, we could do what Simeon Stylites, a Christian in the first century did. Disgusted by the immorality of the world around him, he climbed to the top of a pillar which remained from an abandoned old building. For the next thirty-seven years Simeon stayed up there, praying, fasting regularly, and effectively avoiding the sin of his world (except perhaps for "looking down" on people. Sorry, couldn't resist). He remained on his pillar until his death. But we already know Colliders are not called to hide. We have to live and function in this world so, since becoming a hermit isn't an option, we could opt for the Christian cluster community.

## Circle the Wagons! (Pop Culture as a Cave Dweller)

When we were kids, our dad brainwashed us to love good ol' Western flicks from the 1950s and 1960s. We would rent classics like *The Magnificent Seven* and anything with John "The Duke" Wayne, then mosey on over to the TV room. The movies were as predictable as Joey Gladstone's jokes, with all the staples consistent to that genre: The clean-shaven good guys wore white hats. The bad guys were always in black, sporting a day's stubble of whiskers. A train would be robbed, the cowboys would walk like they still had hangers in their shirts, and there was always an inevitable brawl in the obligatory saloon. To fend off the natives when they attacked their wagon trains, the cowboys would circle the wagons. That way they could effectively keep the women and children in and the bad guys out. From behind a wagon wheel with spokes the width of drinking straws, the hero could take cover and fire several rounds at anyone who got too close.

That's what we Christians often do when we sense danger. We circle the wagons. Cave Dwellers are keenly aware of the damage pop culture can inflict on a good guy's morals. So the fall-back solution is to huddle together and isolate ourselves from the knives and arrows of secular influence. From our safe vantage point, we fire back a few bullets of condemnation, but our primary goal is to protect our own people. That's one reaction we can take to the pop culture menace. Another one is to try to beat the world at its own game.

## It's the Christian Brand

A good argument could be made that our younger sister is, in fact, a first-class diva. However, let's just call her "fashion conscious." To her, "delayed gratification" is however long it takes to drive to the mall. Occasionally, when I (Dan) owe her a favor, I'll be dragged along to a shopping center on one of her ambitious colonizing conquests. Last time we pulled into the mall parking lot, Carrie sighed, "Ah, home sweet home!" (God save me.)

"What are you looking for this time?" I nervously asked, struggling to keep pace.

"Well," she said, her eyes lighting up, "I've narrowed it down to either an article from the Summer Frocks Ready-to-Wear Chanel collection *or* the new patent leather Prada tote bag from Saks. Both are totally chic right now. I want a sophisticated look. But not *too* sophisticated. Mature yet youngish. Classy yet not snobby. What about you?"

"Um, I'm thinking either something green or something blue." OK, so I'm not exactly Giorgio Armani. It can be hard to keep up with brand names. Now we can add a Christian brand to the list.

Like the pigs in George Orwell's *Animal Farm*, we have gradually replaced secular pop culture with our own versions, giving believers Christianized facsimiles for just about everything:

- Guitar Hero becomes Guitar Praise.
- J. K. Rowling is traded in for Francine Rivers.
- AC/DC—out. Hillsong United—in.
- Halloween morphs into Fall Festival.
- *The Notebook* is replaced by *Fireproof.*
- Disney World becomes The Holy Land Experience.
- *High School Musical* changes to *Sunday School Musical.*

In fact, Christian pop culture is even complete with our own superheroes, celebrities, rumors, and gossip!

Now our intent is not to bash Christian material, and in reality a lot of good stuff is produced by Christians these days. For example, even some adamant nonbelievers say Christian bookstores stock the best hard rock music. The movies by Sherwood Pictures continue to impact both Christians and nonbelievers. Then, of course, there is the wonderful little book you are holding in your hands. The fact is certainly not lost on us that we are contributing members to this parallel pop culture. So let's be clear: we're not saying you're a Cave Dweller if you enjoy a Christian book or choose a CD that honors God instead of "the gods of rock." But when we immerse ourselves in Christian subculture as a way to immunize ourselves from the world, we are backing into our cave.

Fortifying ourselves from pop culture to avoid its influence is counterproductive. If we're forced to hide out, then it *is* influencing us. It's like claiming we were unaffected by a nuclear bomb because we spent our entire lives in an underground bunker. Also, there is much culture to appreciate that doesn't have a Christian brand stamped on it. Many forms of literature (especially the classics), film, and music really make you think; they broaden your knowledge about other countries; and they offer eye-opening insights into human nature. Also, it is difficult (or perhaps impossible) to be "in the world" (John 17:18) without knowing what makes the world tick. Mike's philosophy professor in seminary asked on the first day of class, "How many of you believe in the theory of evolution?" Of course no hands went up. These were seminary students after all. Then he asked, "How many of you have read even a page of Charles Darwin's *The Origin of Species*?" Only a couple of brave souls ventured to raise their hands. At that the professor gave some powerful advice: "Don't look down on the world's beliefs in favor of your own if you have no idea what the world actually believes. Would you be frustrated with an atheist who mocked Christianity but had never read a page of the Bible? Don't do the same thing to them." We don't have to be experts in what the world believes, but a general grasp of what's in the media today goes a long way to building bridges with unbelievers. Chances are they will not be familiar with our Christian merchandise, but we can be aware of theirs.

David Platt, pastor of The Church at Brook Hills, came to realize just how "us centered" churches have become. In his book *Radical*, he writes, "We were settling for a Christianity that

> *God didn't send His Son to create a safe Christian empire; He came to turn the existing world on its head.*

revolves around catering to ourselves when the central message of Christianity is actually about denying ourselves."[24] We've created our own comfortable Christian subculture, complete with an abundance of Christian entertainment, so we can more effectively keep our distance from the world. It's all designed and tailor-made for Christians. But when Jesus came in the flesh, why didn't He simply overthrow the existing order and establish a Christian state? Because that was never God's plan. God didn't send His Son to create a safe Christian empire; He came to turn the existing world on its head. If we want to follow Christ's example, we won't merely fill our caves with safe Christian alternatives that keep us from having to venture out. We have been commissioned to transform the world outside the cave.

## It's Greek to Me

I (Dan), have had several (thousand) problems in school. One of which was that I couldn't even spell "foreign language" without access to a good dictionary, let alone learn to speak one. In seventh grade this slight road bump in my academics led my French teacher to magnanimously transfer me out of his class into law without consulting me. By way of explanation, he said, "Daniel, haven't the French already been through enough?" In college my anemic language skills seemed to baffle even the professor. I singlehandedly brought the class average down one letter grade (hey, I wasn't dubbed "sandpaper to the soul" by my profs for nothing). The summer I did refugee work in Greece, my lapse in linguistics would get me into some trouble, or should I say, into some *μεγάλο κόπο*.

I quickly discovered that outdoor flea markets aren't the best place for me. On my first foray I was bombarded by merchants shouting gibberish at me. I stood dazed like a kid standing in Willy Wonka's chocolate factory as objects were piled into my arms, and the friendly merchants kindly counted my money for me. Ten minutes later my wallet was empty, and my arms were full of useless pots, ugly shirts that didn't fit, and several Greek souvenirs made in China. Lesson learned I thought.

I later decided to check out the ancient city of Corinth. After a lengthy train ride I arrived. It was a fascinating place. I toured and explored to my heart's content—so much so I didn't notice when the sun began to set. Suddenly it became imperative I head to the station quickly before the last train departed. Finding an available taxi, I informed the driver I needed a lift to the train depot, making sure to speak in slow English and use animated hand actions. Through broken Greek-lish he informed me he knew a shortcut, shaving twenty minutes off the trip, saving me money as a result.

---

### CULTURE CLIP: *POCAHONTAS*

In the Disney rendition of *Pocahontas*, English settlers land on North American soil and encounter the native tribes. Immediately sizing up these people as only a mission to accomplish, they try forcing them to accept European language and customs. The newcomers are totally oblivious to the rich culture the natives already have. When the natives refuse to capitulate to the English, violence ensues.

In the midst of the struggle, however, a settler named John Smith falls in love with the native princess Pocahontas. She teaches him her culture and he shares his and their bond grows. John Smith learns to love Pocahontas by entering her world. This love is not shared by the rest of his comrades, whose only mission is to conquer and change the native people.

When he pulled over to drop me off, I didn't see a train station, so I asked for confirmation. Spouting out more hurried Greek (or Pharisee, or Arabic, or Elvish for all I knew), he explained that right around the building I would find the train to take me back to Athens. I handed over the fare, which seemed pretty steep, but he kindly helped me count out the proper payment. The taxi sped off (no doubt to catch the bank before closing), and I walked around the building. My jaw dropped and took my heart with it.

It was indeed a train station, but by the looks of it there hadn't been a train through since Alexander the Great's baggage train. The only life forms visible were the spiders hanging from the cobwebs. I had been scammed! I found myself in the most authentic Greek part of Corinth. No one spoke English. My cell phone battery had died, and my wallet was empty (stupid Corinthian flea market). It was getting dark and I was completely stranded. Eighteen years old, alone, tired, broke, hungry, slightly embarrassed, and far from home. I wanted my mommy! Well, thanks to my ability to cry like a six-year-old girl, I was eventually rescued and returned to Athens safe, sound, and sheepish.

## Now You're Speaking My Language!

It's almost impossible to communicate with people if you don't speak their language. Even if they *do* speak English, some subcultures form their own style of speaking as a way of tightening up their sense of community. Anyone who isn't part of the group has little idea what is being said. People who heard, "The ace was completely filthy on the hill as that seeing-eye slider found leather instead of lumber, piling up another 'K' while escaping the pickle and preventing a pair of ribbies and a round tripper. Perhaps the man on deck should sacrifice," might picture a wacky ritual service of expectant mothers who play cards and neglect showers rather than a baseball game.

We were playing ball at a family reunion when our little preschool cousin Elizabeth hit the ball. As the fielders (her uncles) continued to commit error after error, Elizabeth's team realized she had a chance for a home run. "Run home! Run home!" they all yelled in unison. Bug-eyed, she seemed confused by all the yelling. Putting her head down, Elizabeth rounded third base, chugged toward home plate, and bolted right past it. We found her a few minutes later sitting on the front step of her house, very proud of her first home run!

The fact is, pop culture is often the language the world speaks. It dominates their conversation because it pervades their lives. When pop icon Michael Jackson passed away in 2009, it was the topic of conversation in North America for many days. Was this because his death would significantly affect the lives of the people discussing him? No, but his music had such a wide influence that one had to search far and wide to find anyone who *didn't* know who he was. Regardless of class, race, or gender, everyone had MJ's music in common. To be completely unfamiliar with the entertainment saturating the lives of unbelievers will leave us hopelessly unprepared to communicate with them on even the most basic level. We might be well equipped to tell them about Christ, but if we are unable to connect with them on a relational level, we may never even get a conversation started.

Think about this: have you ever invited a classmate to a church social event who had never been to church before? Your friend steps through the door and enters a new world where parties are referred to as fellowships, friends are called "brothers and sisters in Christ," story-telling is known as "sharing your testimony," middle-class people claim to be "children of the King," and people sing about being "washed in the blood"! By the end of the night your friend needs some extra-strength Advil. In fact, we'll confess that sometimes *we* have no idea what's being said. But oftentimes we are happy to let them enter our foreign world to try and figure *us* out but are hesitant to involve ourselves too closely with *their* world.

## Poor Ambassadors

Are your parents getting after you because you are thirty-five, still living in their basement, and unemployed? Fear not. The Bible states that, as Christians, our vocation is to be God's ambassadors

(2 Cor. 5:50). We are *employed* by heaven to represent its goodness in the midst of a decaying world. Now if archangel Gabriel were to analyze how you've spent the past year, what do you think would be written on your annual performance review? Here are some excerpts allegedly taken from job reports:

1. If he were any more stupid, he'd have to be watered twice a week.
2. He donated his brain to science before he was done using it.
3. Some drink from the fountain of knowledge; he only gargled.
4. This employee should go far, and the sooner he starts the better.
5. Since my last report, this employee has reached rock bottom and has started to dig.
6. This employee is depriving a village somewhere of an idiot.

Hopefully none of these are causing déjà vu. But have you ever considered what an ambassador does? To represent your country abroad, you would likely have to learn a new language and adopt foreign customs and traditions. There are places in the world where a gesture of hospitality is to partially chew a nut and then offer it to the guest. Incorrect (but tempting) response: gag, retch, puke, no thanks, I'm allergic.

How long would an ambassador to Africa last if she refused to get off the plane for fear of catching AIDS? "Christian Collider" is really another term for "Christ's Ambassador," which means we don't have the option of blockading ourselves against the pop culture of our generation. It's the world to which we have been sent. Is it safe and cozy? No. The Bible says we are sent into the world as sheep among wolves (Matt. 10:16).

We love to tease Dan's wife Sarah because sometimes it seems she only opens her mouth to exchange feet (figuratively speaking of course). Thankfully, she has no problem poking fun at herself. When she moved to a new city for college, she immediately got involved in a small church. But after six months she was frustrated because her new congregation wasn't as friendly as she thought it should be. One Sunday afternoon she called Dan to rant: "A lady came up this morning and had to ask my *name*," she lamented, "but I've been attending for months and have spoken with her before!" Dan, curious because he visited that church himself, asked what the inconsiderate woman's name was. Sarah responded without hesitation, "Oh I have no idea, I'm *horrible* with names." It's a lot easier to ask others to do something we aren't willing to do in return, isn't it? Responding to pop culture as a Cave Dweller is tempting because it keeps us safely in our comfort zone and beckons others to enter our world. But an effective ambassador has the *responsibility* to communicate effectively with people.

## Overindulged (Experiencing Pop Culture as a Cave-In)

Well, if we've convinced you it's not a good idea to be out of touch with the people of the world we are called to love, we need also to warn you about getting *too* familiar with the world's entertainment. While the goal is to strike a balance of moderation, many of us can instead become completely engulfed by pop culture. There's an intense part in the book *Twilight* (well, as intense as a teen vampire romance novel gets anyway) where Bella has been bitten by a vampire and her blood is poisoned. Her boyfriend (and a hunky vampire himself) Edward Cullen must suck out the poison. However, he is hesitant to do so, knowing that due to his vampire nature, it will be hard for him to stop himself once he has started, and he could kill her.

Once we've had a taste of what the world offers, we can become addicted, filling our lives to overflowing with shallow entertainment. We rock in Trivial Pursuit because we know the answers to pointless questions. We subscribe to several different celebrity gossip magazines. We play RPG games across the Internet, own countless movies, religiously follow our favorite sports teams, and have iPods crammed with three times the music we actually listen to. When we get so engrossed in pop culture that it becomes the standard for our opinions and decisions, we have caved in and become too close with the world.

## "It Doesn't Affect Me" (Yeah, right!)

Both of us have always had a propensity to really get into the entertainment we enjoy. After watching a spy thriller, we were busted by our mom for dusting our car for fingerprints (but Mom, they're after us!). And yes, we have attended midnight movie premieres dressed in full costume. So we'd be the last ones to suggest that media has no effect on us. We didn't just *watch* Teenage Mutant Ninja Turtles as kids—we *were* Leonardo and Raphael.

Let's not deceive ourselves: the movies we rent, the books we read, the music we listen to, and even the conversations we have about such entertainment all influence us. The real question is what kind of impact it will have. We had a friend who constantly talked about the latest shoot 'em up action flick he watched. We knew that many of the movies he rattled off contained ridiculous amounts of sex, violence, and cursing (not to mention dangerous philosophies and twisted worldviews), so we asked him if that was the best thing to be filling his mind. He simply shrugged off our concern and said, "It's OK; that stuff doesn't affect me." But it *does* affect us. It is scary how often we casually flip past a news story of a natural disaster or terrorist attacks on TV. CNN could be showing us dead bodies littering the streets of Iraq, but all we have to do is change the channel if we don't want to see it anymore. There was a time when scenes like this were shocking, but now many of us have seen much worse on the big screen while munching buttered popcorn. We must be careful not to let pop culture jade us toward the important things of life. There is a *real* battle raging all around us, and it is for the souls of our friends, family, and coworkers; and they need us to love them more than we love our entertainment choices.

## Would You Like That Crispy?

The bright sun rays warmly bathed my body, and the rhythmic pulse of crashing waves lulled me gently into dreamland. It was Spring Break! I (Dan) had never been to Myrtle Beach before, and I was amazed I had lived so long without experiencing this heavenly utopia. Closing my eyes, I thought: *Can life get any better than this?* Perhaps not, but as I awoke the next morning, I discovered it could get worse. *Much* worse.

I grew up enduring the epic-long winters on the western plains of Canada where there are only two seasons: eleven months of winter and one month of bad skiing. Ask Canadians what they do in the summer, and they'll say, "Well, if it falls on a Saturday, we throw a picnic!" My pale skin was long deprived of sunlight. I vowed to make the most of the beach, soaking up Vitamin D like a ShamWow does water. So when my mom handed me a bottle of sunscreen, I quickly declined, "Thanks, Mom, but no thanks. I don't want anything standing between this bod and a quick olive-oil tan. Besides, I *never* burn!" So, after a day of snoozing on the beach, I crawled into bed that night satisfied I was well on my way to a bronzed Zeus-like body. Comfortable I drifted into sleep, excited to hit the beach again the next day.

"*Ahhh!*" Our condo was on fire! I must rescue the women from the inferno! I tried to leap out of bed, but a searing pain paralyzed me. Wait! The building wasn't burning up. *I* was! I opened my eyes, expecting to see my bed covered by boiling lava. I am no Sherlock Holmes, but as I gingerly lifted the covers, I could readily deduce the source of my agony. A rosy-cheeked lobster had donned a pair of red-swim shorts, bathed in tomato paste, and crawled into my bed. Either that or I was burned to a crisp. There wasn't a fraction of an inch of my body that wasn't glowing like Rudolph's nose. Even my fingernails felt warm.

### Aftereffects

Experience is a great teacher. Two jumbo bottles of aloe vera lotion later, and Dan was shedding so much epidermis our mom covered the furniture with sheets. He realized an important life lesson (besides the one any four-year-old could have told him about SPF protection): pleasures that lull you into checking out mentally can hurt you.

The impact of media is so gradual and it comes from so many

directions we don't even feel the collision. Like Dan, we can be enjoying ourselves, minding our own business and remain completely unaware we are being assaulted by the very things we are using to pamper ourselves. Dan paid for his inattention with a sunburn to trump all sunburns. Let's look at a few ways pop culture can burn us if we're careless.

### Messed-Up Relationships

Where do teenagers get their model for how to handle a relationship? Chick flicks (*ahem,* or so we're told) are mostly variations of the classic Disney theme (think Cinderella). They cover the *falling* in love (time span, one waltz), but they don't concern themselves too much with the *staying* in love. Sit-coms show relationships with enough chemistry to blow up Frankenstein's lab but have little or no substance. Romance novels are heavy on the bodice ripping, but once the bodices have been ripped, there's not much else to them. Teen mags and gossip rags focus on . . . well, let's not even go there. So, if you were to describe what a loving,

> ### CULTURE CLIP: *ANTONY AND CLEOPATRA*
>
> Shakespeare's renowned play tells the story of Antony, an appointed Roman leader. To reestablish stability he embarks to Egypt as an ambassador.
>
> Once there he is sucked into the Egyptian culture's extravagant luxury and pleasures, not the least of which is the love of its queen, Cleopatra.
>
> Antony grows indifferent to the fate of Rome, sidetracked by the Egyptian culture. When an eventual battle materializes between the two countries, Antony leads the attack against his former land.

lasting, godly relationship looks like, what would you say? Do we even know what true love is? How is a kid brought up in a broken home supposed to learn about love that goes the distance? From a reality show? Why is the teen pregnancy rate alarmingly high? Could it be that young girls are trying to experience love the way the party crowd does on *Friends*? Or maybe they just want to have some fun a la *Sex and the City*. Unfortunately, we often get the news flash that life is not a sit-com once we've already damaged our relationships (and reputations) beyond repair.

### Stupid Choices

A second by-product of TV Land is the dangerous choices made by undiscerning viewers (hence the brilliant marketing scheme known as the disclaimer *Viewer Discretion Advised*. Could there be a better way to lure in a guy?) Why is there not a beer commercial where the buffed guy has to hold back the gorgeous girl's ponytail as she pukes her guts into the toilet? Or a magazine ad for cologne that shows a dude with a muffin top and a weak chin? Radio host Michael Medved observed "in a nation in which the average citizen watches the tube for close to thirty hours a week, the characters on the small screen serve to define what constitutes normal and desirable behavior."[25] We think our own life should be just like

---

### COLLIDER BIO: ALICE COOPER

Although Cooper (born Vincent Damon Furnier) grew up in church, he soon abandoned it in pursuit of his musical dreams. He eventually found them when his band hit the peak of their success in the 1970s.

Alice is still considered one of the most influential rockers of all time, selling millions of records and becoming a pioneer for theatrical "shock rock." He had it all until alcohol began to ruin his life. He was living the dream, but it left him unfulfilled.

Although he had never completely abandoned his belief in God, he came to the realization that Jesus must be Lord. He turned his life over to Christ and watched his record sales plummet as news of his faith hit the public media. But that didn't matter, for he had finally seen past the world's lies.

In his autobiography he writes: "Ultimately, becoming a Christian became the most rebellious and risky thing I've ever done. I was now rebelling against the very business that had invented me, and that's true rebellion. Who's the biggest rebel to ever live? Jesus Christ." (Cooper 2007)

the world we see through the magical lens of our TV or computer screen, and when it doesn't turn out that way, we don't know what to do.

### Squandered Hours (or Days)

A third side effect of pop culture is our wasted time. TV shows and video games can eat away hours of a day. And now, thanks to technology, we never have to miss our favorite show or game. If we have to head out to class or work, we can record hours of missed entertainment for when we get home.

Both of us are what you might call obsessive personality types. We discovered this when we were introduced to the show *LOST.* The problem was, it was currently the sixth and final season. We had some catching up to do before the finale. Several all-nighters, bloodshot eyes, and eleven-episode days later we completed the epic journey, just in time for the series finale. How many hours was that? It's embarrassing to consider what opportunities we may have missed during that time just to watch a finale we could have recorded anyway. In fact, the DVR recording schedule at our house can often be more complicated than Riemann hypothesis. It's not just what Tinseltown puts *into* us that affects us; it's what it takes *away*—the valuable, irreplaceable commodity called *time*. The words "I don't have time" should never come from the mouth of a person who watches even one TV show an evening. The problem isn't always *time* but *priorities*. Speaking of which . . .

### Sidetracked Priorities

Surely Satan is a football fan (probably cheers for the Dallas Cowboys, just kidding). Sunday afternoon games are perfectly timed. What better way to relax before the crazy workweek? And what better way to get Christians to dash home from church, become engrossed in a game, and forget all about the encounter with God that took place during worship service?

When you and your friends get together, what do you talk about? The newest movies coming to theaters? Favorite bands? What insightful knowledge do you glean from the pages of *Entertainment Weekly?*

Something like this? "After a long-term (two-month) relationship, Celeb A got married to Celeb B but had an affair with Celeb C, who was Celeb D's ex, (but was recently photographed at the beach with Celeb E). Now Celeb A is enjoying single parenting, and Celebs B and C are enjoying an alternate-lifestyle relationship. " The old cliché says, "What goes in must come out." This adage was proven true when our buddy Caleb attempted to down a baker's dozen Krispy Kreme doughnuts in a five-minute span. It's also true that when we cram our brains with pop culture. That's what will dominate our thoughts and conversations. Jesus said the things we put into our hearts will come out in our actions (Matt. 15:16–19).

## Summary

Pop culture is a complicated road to trek. We don't want to sound too negative because we obviously enjoy much of what pop culture has to offer. We have our favorite shows, bands, movies, games, and books just like you. However, we are still learning just how easy it is for Satan to lure us into a snare through our entertainment choices. The unfortunate part is that we often do most of the work for him. We allow the godless worldview into our lives in our unguarded moments but try to balance it out with little from God.

So, what's the best thing to do? If we don't want to hide away in Christian culture and we don't want to soak in the world's entertainment like a sponge, is there any other option? Yes! The collision of pop culture doesn't have to deliever a crippling impact. Now that we've talked about how we can defend ourselves against Satan's poison gas attacks, in the next section we will learn how to fire back. We may only be a small group preparing to collide against a thunderous wave, but if God is our strength, He can use us to think critically through the entertainment all around us and maybe just make a difference while we're at it. Read on to see how a Collider can impact pop culture and turn Satan's own weapon against him.

## SO WHAT?

1. When do you most often indulge in entertainment? When you are tired or bored? When you are spending time with your friends or family? When you are alone?

2. How many hours do you spend enjoying entertainment choices? How many hours do you spend with God or serving others? Is there a noticeable difference in the time allotments?

3. How do you think your entertainment choices affect you? When you think of relationships, what comes to mind? Have you found yourself acting or talking like the people you've seen on TV? Do you wish the world was more like it is in the movies?

## WHAT NOW?

1. Keep a log for one week of how many hours you spend listening to music, going to movies, or watching TV. Do the results surprise you?

2. Choose one entertainment choice in your life and go a week (or longer) without it. Replace it with something else (like reading your Bible, reading a Christian book, serving others, volunteering at your church). Did you miss it? What did this experiment teach you about yourself? Do you really need that form of distraction in your life, or should you cut back from it a little bit?

3. This week, choose something you see or hear in your entertainment and find out what God thinks of it. It might be the way characters in a movie interact, a lyric from a song, or a statement made in a novel. Dig into your Bible and talk with your friends, parents, or pastor about it. Can you see the difference between the world's values and God's? What did this teach you about God?

Chapter 9

## REVERSING THE COLLISION—
## USING POP CULTURE AS A TOOL

*Amid the various cultures and subcultures of the world,
an all-embracing, all-transcending reality has been
established which—even more than popular culture—
cuts across, infiltrates, pervades, and will ultimately
overwhelm and supplant all others. This is the
presence—and culture—of the kingdom of God.*[26]
—T. M. MOORE (CHRISTIAN AUTHOR AND CULTURAL CRITIC)

*Well, I think I've lived long enough to see the
world change, and I do believe in a real way that
we live in Playboy world now.*[27]
—HUGH HEFNER (FOUNDER OF *PLAYBOY*)

### Does This Shirt Make Me Look Fat?

When you're a fan of rock music, you wear T-shirts of your
favorite bands. I (Mike) don't know what brilliant marketing guru
started this trend, but for years rockers and wannabe rockers alike

have proudly sported threads of their musical heroes. I remember the day I entered the fray. I had never bought band merchandise over the Internet before and didn't understand why they needed so much information. ("If you were stranded on a desert island with the choice of only one breakfast cereal . . .") But I filled in all the necessary blanks and excitedly clicked the Submit Order button. Then the waiting began (Note: I am notoriously terrible at waiting).

Eagerly I checked the mailbox every single day (sometimes several times a day). The days stretched into weeks, and just when I concluded Canada Post switched to dog-sled to be more environmentally friendly, it arrived. I called a family meeting for the ceremonial opening of the package and feverishly ripped into it to reveal a shirt sized XXXX Small. My disappointment turned to denial, and I attempted to squeeze my teenage torso into that tiny piece of doll clothing. When my arms started turning blue from lack of blood flow, I turned to my mom and sighed, "Mom, my life is just a series of disappointments!" I soon got tired of that band anyway.

---

**CULTURE CLIP: *THE DEATH OF IVAN ILYCH***

In the book *The Death of Ivan Ilych*, the great Russian novelist Leo Tolstoy gave a haunting depiction of a life wasted.

Protagonist Ivan Ilych is likable and successful. He lives out his days engaging in whatever the world has to offer and spends his energy climbing the social ladder.

However, he suddenly discovers he is dying. As he lies on his deathbed, he looks back on his life and realizes he has not lived well, investing in things that have no eternal significance.

---

## Where Moth and Rust Destroy

When Christ enters your life, He flips your world around. As a spiritually new creation, you are so radically transformed the trappings of this world no longer satisfy you. Your mood no longer rests on who's been voted off the Island, or who is "safe" on *American*

*Idol* (but, for the record, Mike called the AI winner three years in a row). The fleeting thrills and entertainment of this world are still diverting, but now they show up for what they really are—temporary. A Christian has to find a balance and synergy between faith and pop culture. The Bible warns us not to store our treasures on earth because they are only momentary (Matt. 6:19).

How much of our time, money, and energy are poured into things that have no lasting significance? (Anyone interested in purchasing a used seven-season set of *Gilmore Girls*?)

Why do we seek to be refreshed by things of the world that will only make us thirstier? This world pushes plenty of short-term thrills, but amusement, adrenaline, and entertainment can never fill the void only God can fill. Country music legend Johnny Cash, who experienced all the temptations and excesses of fame, said, "I know from experience that I'm happiest when I'm closest to Him, so it's no mystery why Bible study pleases me so. It's one of the ways I get to the well."[28] Let God guide us in how we navigate through pop culture. *He* is our Lord; Hollywood is not.

## Discerning Eyes—a Collider's Response

Chances are, if you've been in school for any period of time, you've been dragged on a field trip to the local Water Treatment Plant (because nothing says fun and educational like dirty polluted water). The building is usually dark and it smells like . . . well, you know what. And after an enlightening tour, you probably spent the next several days in a state of severe dehydration.

Being a Collider in the midst of pop culture's bombardment actually requires similar action to those treatment plants where the vile, polluted water is miraculously filtered into a state worthy of drinking. Dan spent an eye-opening two weeks with a team of doctors and nurses traveling along the Amazon River to take medical help to remote Brazilian villages. The natives, unaware of the health hazard, would fill their water jugs from the river in front of their house. Meanwhile, their upstream neighbors would empty their sewer and garbage into that same river. That lack of knowledge caused the villagers horrific disease and malnutrition.

Everything produced by pop culture is not bad. Everything you see on TV or read in a secular book won't rot your brain, so Christians don't have to overreact and hide away from pop culture. On the other hand, it's foolish to gobble up blindly everything pop culture throws your way. We should filter pop culture through our relationship with Christ. What forms of entertainment honor Him? This doesn't mean we *only* watch TV preachers and listen to *Adventures in Odyssey*, but we can be proactive about our choices rather than passively absorbing whatever *pollution* comes along. A few things to consider regarding an entertainment option: Will your values be assaulted by the end of the hour, or will you be challenged and provoked to think? Will your choice provide a clearer insight into the world or insult your intelligence with vulgar and crude sewage?

The world hurls its stuff at you hour by hour, day by day, making collisions inevitable. Realizing that much of what pop culture throws your way is garbage, what should you do? Well, you can move to a cloistered Amish community (incredible food but limited fashion choices). Or you can open the floodgates and splash around in whatever sludge comes along. Caving in (taking it all in with no filter) makes you a person of no spiritual influence while cave dwelling removes you from any possible place where you could make a difference. But you can make pop culture work for you as a source of recreation and good entertainment and also as a tool for serving God. That's the Collider's response. If you spend time with God, praying and studying the Bible, you'll learn to be discerning and to think carefully through the things you allow into (and block out of) your life. Then you can master pop culture rather than giving it mastery over you.

## What about Holiness?

The Bible tells us not to conform to the pattern of this world (Rom. 12:2). We're not called to point a judging finger at others, nor are we restricted only to watching VeggieTales, but we *are* called to a higher code of conduct. We shouldn't be shocked that nonbelievers flock to the latest raunchy comedy or fill their ears with profanity-laced music. Those are the world's standards, and they are people of the world. But Christ has called us to live by a different set of principles. An article entitled "Movies, Money, & God" in *Entertainment Weekly* noted the growing relationship between Christians and the movie industry saying, "Young Christians are embracing mainstream movies—not just blockbusters . . . but unlikely films . . . that might have horrified their grandparents."[29]

Chances are we've all seen movies and sung along to a few songs we knew were questionable. Birthday parties, especially sleepovers, were land mines when we were younger. Inevitably out comes a movie you know you'd never watch at home. So you either make a scene, fake a stomachache and go home, or sit for two hours while your conscience pleads with you to reconsider.

We need to encourage one another to live on a higher plane. It's hard to be the only one standing up for what's right, but we've learned from experience that most of the time others feel the same way; they're just reluctant to take the lead. Colliders are the ones who muster the guts to say something. If your friends select offensive DVD rentals, be the one who suggests another option, or plan to meet them after the movie. If you're driving with your buddies and a trashy song comes on the radio, start up a conversation instead. Not only will you be discerning in what you let into your head, chances are you'll encourage others to follow your example. We don't have control over what media the world throws out, but we can choose what gets through our filter. By being smart, we can change the atmosphere around us.

Isn't it ironic we pay money to be offended? Does God's call to live holy lives (1 Pet. 1:14–15) really mean so little to us that we'll dish out $10 for a movie that celebrates the very things that break God's heart? We would never hand a stranger a crisp twenty to mock and ridicule our boyfriend/girlfriend, but we don't think twice about doing that to

God. Life is more than this. As Christian Colliders, let's think long and hard about our entertainment choices. It's hard to find media choices that don't have *something* questionable, but we can readily rule out some serious no-brainers. One thing we can know for sure: Christ did not go to the cross so we could fill our lives with frivolous hours of mind-numbing or degrading "entertainment." The collision with pop culture takes down so many young Christians because they ditch holiness in their craving for acceptance. Or, they're simply careless in the way they spend their leisure time. We're supposed to stand out from the world around us. Let's invest our time in pursuing God and loving people; these are the things that really matter. Christian colliding is not just about surviving the impact; it's also about colliding back.

## Action!

Colliders experience pop culture in an inverted way from our non-Christian peers. The world tells us just to "kick back, relax the mind, and enjoy the show." But that's not the time to zone out or put our minds in neutral.

> Let's invest our time in loving God and loving people; these are the things that really matter.

Let's *think* about what we watch and listen to. For example, when the two of us saw the blockbuster hit *Avatar*, we didn't just munch on our popcorn for two hours (or five, or six, or however long it was) and then forget about it. We talked about it afterward. Oddly enough, *Avatar* actually related in a big way to the way Christians approach sharing their faith with other cultures. The humans in James Cameron's film, driven by their own ambitions and conquests, were only out to change the culture of the alien Na'vi; they had no compassion for them. Isn't that disturbingly similar to the way North Americans sometimes approach evangelism and missions?

By now you'll have noticed several "Culture Clips" in this book. We included them to show you some ways Colliders can interact with pop culture. It really boils down to one word: *think*. Know what's going on around the world; read about countries where poverty and war are everyday realities, not just backdrops for love stories. Guys, let's make it obvious to everyone in the room that we are *not* glued to the screen when a commercial comes on featuring women wearing next to nothing or the camera zooms in on the cheerleaders during halftime. This needs to be our response even when we are alone, but we can promise you the girls you know will especially appreciate your doing this when you're with them. And don't forget your remote has a fast-forward button on it. Why are we so hesitant to use it? Trust us, nobody will take away your birthday when you refuse to be subjected to immorality, and despite what film directors believe, you'll still be able to enjoy the movie *without* that two-minute sex scene.

## Sweeping Out the Cobwebs

The world continues to dumb things down for our generation. The quick-witted humor of *The Dick Van Dyke Show* and *The Cosby Show* has been replaced by crude jokes and witless routines. Musicians used to sing about pivotal issues in the world; now they blather about partying in clubs or profanely rap about violence, degrade women, and brag about jail time. Let's not insult ourselves by dropping to that level. There's actually a lot of good being produced if we only navigate our way around the sketchy stuff and stretch our minds a little.

For instance, when's the last time you've opened a book? Despite what you might have heard, reading isn't just for old people (or boring Lit majors like Dan)! Like all pop culture, there are good books and garbage books, but literature has the power to challenge us and make us think more than most of the television shows we routinely fall back to. Classic books such as Bradbury's *Fahrenheit 451* and Turgenev's *Fathers and Sons* will make you think about the power of ideas and what's really important in life while providing suspenseful thrills equal to anything showing in the theater. Stowe's *Uncle Tom's Cabin* will impact the way you look at racism. Remarque's *All Quiet on the Western Front* will undoubtedly give you new appreciation for our troops. You can even learn some shocking World War II history through the comic panels of Art Spiegelman's *Maus*. There are some great, well-written books that will strengthen your faith as well, such as *Mere Christianity* by C. S. Lewis, *The Cross and the Switchblade* by David Wilkerson, or *The Cost of Discipleship* by Dietrich Bonhoeffer. A good mix of secular and Christian literature will keep you grounded while allowing you to see the world in a new way. We're not expecting that *everyone* will become geeky bookworms like us, but you might just find that your brain enjoys the shake-up in a normally electronic-dominated schedule. Whereas TV and movies generally showcase the world's morals, literature captures the world's philosophies, which can prove invaluable to connecting with its people.

---

### COLLIDER BIO: THE BROWN FAMILY

Mark and Angie and their two daughters Meagan and Erin (along with Erin's husband Stuart) are not your typical Christian ministry group. Their outreach tool? Good old-time rock 'n' roll!

As a young man, Mark was realizing his dream. His band was quickly rising, and a record deal was on the table. He should have been happy, but he was miserable. That day he turned his musical talents over to God. Years later God has rewarded him for that decision.

Mark and his musical family formed Brown Family Ministries in 2009. They sold their house, bought an RV, and now travel, performing classic rock favorites at rodeos, town festivals, and local block parties. They use their music to build relationships with some hard-living individuals, such as bull riders and recovering substance abusers in halfway houses. Through their music they mingle with a people group who might never seek out a church. God is using this ordinary family (with extraordinary music skills) in amazing ways to build bridges and point people to Christ.

"Classic rock music is a nonthreatening relationship builder that allows our family to get to know people and show them the love of Christ." —Mark Brown, www.brownfamilyministries.org

---

### How Poetic

The apostle Paul was a model Christian Collider. Having been dramatically converted to Christianity himself, he skillfully used his knowledge about the prevalent values in his day to gain an audience with the polytheistic Greek people of the first century. Paul made reference to several Greek poets (basically the celebrities back then) and showed how even their secular poetry pointed to the one true God (Acts 17:22–31).

A few years ago we attended Vans Warped Tour, a secular rock festival that travels throughout the United States and Canada. With six stages simultaneously spotlighting punk-rock bands, there seemed to be a not-so-covert competition among the musicians to see who could drop the most F-bombs during a thirty-minute set. However, several Christian bands were also featured, and they stood out as light in the darkness. Artists such as Underoath, Haste the Day, and Family Force Five boldly spoke the name of Jesus from the stage, and they also drew some of the largest crowds. While some would criticize them for playing such a worldly festival, these bands realized how valuable music can be as a tool to connect people to Jesus. In each concert they boldly represented Christ to thousands of people in a setting where many might fear to tread. What they were doing is the very thing Jesus Himself did. He too was chastised, not just for hanging out with sinners but for doing it on their turf. He reminded His critics, "Those who are well don't need a doctor, but the sick do need one. I didn't come to call the righteous, but sinners" (Mark 2:17).

So, if you're thinking, *I have no credibility because I'm not a scholar/orator like Paul or in a face-melting Christian rock band*, be encouraged! The point is, *anyone* can think critically and biblically about the media they inhale. If we are aware of what the Bible says about relationships, we won't have to take our cues from Nicholas Sparks. To be a Collider is a call to infiltrate the pop culture of our world, not to create our own parallel one. C. S. Lewis wisely noted, "What we want is not more little books about Christianity, but more little books by Christians on other subjects with their Christianity *latent*."[30]

We once witnessed an amusing spectacle at McDonalds. A man, frustrated after having his order messed up, tossed up his hands and proclaimed to the whole room, "That's it! I'm never eating here *ever* again!" He then stormed out the doors, right under the sign reading "billions and billions served." He really showed *them*! Let's be realistic, we are not going to overthrow Hollywood. No matter how many things we boycott or protest against, Hollywood is going to continue doing big business. That doesn't mean we can't have an impact on it. Pop culture is in the veins of the world; it is what connects people. When Christians dare to enter the system, rather than hiding from it or imitating it, they tap into the pulse of a culture in need of the fresh perspective only Christ can give. The more Christians pursue God's standards instead of secular standards, the more we will change the way people *think*. In fact, this could be more important than all the Christian entertainment being produced, for if you change the way people *think*, you change the way they act and the way they live. Don't think that just because you cannot transform Hollywood you can't affect the people around you. What kind of influence are you having on your friends? Perhaps the furthest your personal influence reaches is simply your group of friends. Let God use that. You may not be able to stop the next graphic movie from being made, but you can be the one who leads by example and encourages your pocket of friends not

---

## CULTURE CLIP: THE TROJAN HORSE

The battle of Troy, as told in Virgils' famous epic *The Aeneid*, was a ten-year stalemate. The towering walls of the fortified Trojan city easily repelled all attempted sieges.

The attacking forces eventually realized the city could not be taken from the outside. The great tactician Odysseus organized the construction of a massive wooden horse to be presented to the king of Troy, allegedly as a gift of surrender. The gift was greedily accepted, and it was quickly brought into the city. Unbeknown to the Trojans, fifty spies were hidden in the belly of the gift.

That night, under cover of darkness, the spies crawled out and opened the gates, allowing the attacking forces in. Troy was captured from the inside.

to be lured in to watch it. You never know what God might do through you as you step out and live a life of integrity. Let your life be like a flashlight, not just to draw attention to the way *you* live but to help navigate others through the darkness as well.

## Stand Up

When we moved from Canada to South Carolina, the two of us packed up Mike's car, kidnapped our cousin JP, and embarked on a crazy six-day road trip (thank goodness for Red Bull). We had numerous adventures on the drive. We visited the famous Mount Rushmore, got stuck in America's biggest biker convention, and locked ourselves out of (and our cell phones into) our car in The-Middle-of-Nowhere, Montana. But perhaps one of the most interesting things we saw

---

### COLLIDER BIO: WILLIAM WILBERFORCE

It's hard for a person living in the twenty-first century to envision the world Wilberforce lived in (nineteenth-century Britain), since it was so unlike modern times. The idea of slavery today makes people cringe, but that was not so in his day. Slavery was not only considered normal; it was *acceptable*. The fact that modern society cannot comprehend such a mind-set is a testimony to the incredible influence of Wilberforce.

Abolishing slavery was unthinkable in Wilberforce's day, and so he faced steep opposition at even suggesting it. But he didn't let that deter him. When he started out, he probably didn't anticipate it would take over twenty years to see his vision become a reality. He literally devoted his life to ending slavery, and he received news of its abolition in 1833 while on his deathbed.

Wilberforce dedicated himself to right a wrong in his society. He was an exceptionally talented individual, whom many believed could have been the prime minister of England had he walked that path. But instead Wilberforce, a committed Christian, realized God could use him to change the way his generation viewed the cruel debacle that slavery truly was.

---

was in Nashville. Right in the heart of Broadway downtown we found Billy Joe's tattoo parlor. We stepped inside to take a look. A big "No Cussing" sign told us this wasn't your average ink shop. We discovered the parlor was actually run entirely by Christians. Billy Joe (the owner) and his wife started the parlor in 2004 with the goal that even in a primarily secular industry and a city filled with ungodly entertainment, they could be shining lights for Christ for people who may never step inside a church building. Billy Joe is an in-your-face kind of guy, who'll share his love for Christ with you no matter who you are. For the last decade many people have left with a lot more than just a sweet ink job.

What about us? How can we use pop culture as a tool to collide for Christ? Dan's wife Sarah is enormously artistically talented. She spent several years at an art school to develop her skills. In an environment dominated by liberal New Age belief, Sarah was determined to represent Jesus to her classmates. For one assignment they were to create a piece of art and present it to the class. As her classmates developed paintings filled with erotic images, Sarah seized her opportunity. When her turn came to present, she unveiled a painting depicting Jesus' journey to the cross and resurrection

---

## COLLIDER BIO: DOUG VAN PELT

In 1985, Van Pelt created *Heaven's Metal* magazine to focus on the heavier side of the Christian music industry. It eventually became so popular he changed the name to *HM* (which now stands for "Hard Music") magazine in 1995.

Although the magazine primarily covers Christian artists, Van Pelt began a feature called "What So-and-So Says" in which he interviews a mainstream secular band. The interview covers many of the expected questions, except two that appear every time: "What do you think about Jesus Christ?" and "What do think about His claim to be the Way the Truth and the Life, and no one comes to the Father except through Him?" Using this outlet, Van Pelt and his writers have had the opportunity to witness to bands such as Godsmack, Kiss, Greenday, Metallica, Nickleback, Drowning Pool, Rage Against the Machine, and many more. "What So-and-So Says" has become the most popular feature of the magazine, as Van Pelt continues to infiltrate the secular music industry. Many of these interviews have been collected in a book entitled *Rock Stars on God: 20 Artists Speak Their Minds about Faith.*

and shared how her own life was impacted by His journey. Sarah not only withstood a hard collision, but she fired back.

I (Dan) spent my first two years of college at a secular, liberal university where the faculty adamantly espoused atheism. One poetry professor was especially vocal, openly challenging God to fistfights and blatantly mocking Him. When he gave an assignment to analyze the lyrics of a song and present your opinion to the class, I chose a Christian song. Thankfully he didn't burn me at the stake, and it was a built-in opportunity to present a Christian perspective to a class that had endured a semester of blasphemy. Popular culture doesn't hesitate to shove a godless worldview in your face so don't be ashamed or timid to push back. Leave the obnoxious bashing to them, but seize the opportunities to stand up for your faith and turn the tables. We've simply got to change our focus from merely wanting to be entertained to wanting God to use us.

## Summary

There's no better tool than pop culture for connecting with and understanding unbelievers. No matter how many protests and boycotts we organize, Christians may never completely transform Hollywood, but that doesn't mean we have to give it power over us. Imagine a battle in which the soldiers played with live hand grenades in their own barracks. All the enemy would have to do is to wait for them to blow themselves up. Likewise, we do Satan's work for him by voluntarily bringing explosives right into our homes.

God has called you to live an exhilarating life with Christ, so don't be content to settle for shallow entertainment. Get into God's Word whenever you can. The Bible will make you think like no other work of literature could. God will give you power to collide in the face of the overwhelming influence of pop culture. Enjoy and appreciate art for what it is, and do your part to contribute, but do so with discretion. Never turn your brain off while taking in entertainment, and remember whom you represent because that is far more important than a forty-five-minute span of whatever reality show or medical drama happens to be popular. Let's stand up and collide with the world of entertainment. Doing so will send Satan running when he realizes his secret grip on our generation is not so secret anymore, and his own arrows are coming volleying back on him.

## SO WHAT?

1. What do you spend your time doing? Are you storing up treasures on earth or heaven?
2. Are most of your entertainment choices Christian or secular? In what ways is this good/bad, and in what ways might you need to find a healthy and productive balance? What is the danger of filling your life with too much of either one?
3. Try to think of an area of life pop culture *hasn't* influenced. In what ways have you seen pop culture's influence? How can this awareness better prepare you for colliding with pop culture?

## WHAT NOW?

1. The next time you watch a movie or TV show, take some time afterward to discuss it with your friends. What can you learn? What does God say about the content, issues, worldviews, and statements?
2. The next time you chat with a friend who doesn't know Jesus, find ways to use pop-culture topics to illustrate spiritual truth. Intentionally engage your friends in valuable conversations about real-life issues.
3. If you're not usually a reader, try starting a book this week. Ask your youth or college pastor to recommend one, or pick up one we've mentioned. Switch out one of your regular time slots of watching TV for reading. Did you enjoy it? Did you feel more energized than you did when you sat in front of a screen? What did you learn?

**Part 5**

# COLLIDING WITH YOUR LIFE

## Chapter 10

# COLLIDING HEAD-ON WITH THE WORLD'S PRIORITIES

*We are half-hearted creatures, fooling about with drink and sex and ambition when infinite joy is offered us, we are like ignorant children who want to continue making mud pies in a slum because we cannot imagine what is meant by the offer of a vacation at the sea. We are far too easily pleased.*[31]
—C. S. LEWIS (CHRISTIAN APOLOGIST AND AUTHOR)

*The only thing that could spoil a day [is] people. People [are] always the limiters of happiness.*[32]
—ERNEST HEMINGWAY (AMERICAN WRITER AND JOURNALIST)

### It Shall Be a Duel . . . to the Death!

Basement cleaning day—the mere mention sends shivers down the spine. The year was 1994. The setting: a dimly lit basement. The scene: a young boy and his siblings, slaving away under the oppressive tyranny of their parents. I was that boy. This is my tale.

Every gloomy Saturday morning I (Dan) rose at sunup and, together with Mike and Carrie, trudged the long sinister staircase—deep, deep into the basement that, without fail, resembled a nuclear testing ground. Sweat dripping from our little brows, we toiled at the monumental task of cleaning up our own mess until the work was completed, and then we graciously accepted an entire *one*-dollar reward. Innocent waifs, we were totally unenlightened to the sick and twisted operation our parents were running.

Being a rather lazy six-year-old, however, I put my mind to other things to pass the time such as tying three-year-old Carrie to the doorknob with her skipping rope and tormenting Mike with dead spiders (the proverbial chink in his otherwise impenetrable armor).

Dad, suspecting the hours worked didn't quite match the progress, began inspecting every so often with the taunting threat of withholding our hard-earned dollar should ever we be discovered idle. The solution was simple; fool around until the sound of footsteps cued me to return to work. Problem solved.

One morning, too lazy to clean, I decided to duel my brother to the death. Grabbing a plastic sword, I yelled, "Have at thee, yonder coward! Or dost thou be chicken?!" Whirling to face me, Mike seized a sword of his own. I smirked, "Ha! So thou art brave indeed! I grant ye that. But death shall floweth quickly from this blade!" But then, for some reason (perhaps the way my sword danced like John Travolta through the air), Mike's eyes bulged and he collapsed to his knees. Realizing victory was within grasp, I leaped onto our toy table. "Ah! Ye whimpering pup! Eat blade!" Then I heard a deep cough.

I spun around to face my dad—my 6 foot 2 inch dad—staring down with a rather stern demeanor. The scam was up. Gulping, I mustered up one last bit of courage. "Dad, you may take my dollar, but you can never take my *freedom*!"

Oh man, what a spanking.

## How Will We Spend It?

Isn't it interesting that despite dizzying scientific and technological advances, humanity has never managed to gain mastery over the clock? The hours race by just as they have for centuries. There are still twenty-four hours in a day, just as there were in medieval times. Modern medicine might prolong your life for a year or two more than your ancestors lived, but we will all eventually die one day. American writer Ernest Hemingway said, "Every man's life ends the same way. It is only the details of how he lived and how he died that distinguish one man from another."[33]

We may give little thought to the unfolding of time, but the fact is every passing second we are investing our lives in something. As the minutes add up to hours and the hours to days, the question is what that investment will be. Will we create a life of achievement or of disappointment? Will our days be filled with joy or with boredom? Will the years be fulfilling or disappointing? Will we be encouragers or complainers, givers or takers? The clock collides

> Many people have no idea how precious their life is until they have already squandered it.

with us every day, and we continuously have to decide how to spend the minutes allotted to us. God's Word has volumes to say about what to do with the days we have been given.

Imagine yourself sixty years from now. You are elderly and wrinkled (Botox was just a fad). You sit in your favorite chair, drinking prune juice. Many of your friends are gone. As you watch the young people scurrying past your house heading for the park or riding their bikes, you recall those sunny summer days of youth filled with so much potential and energy. Back then your life lay before you like an empty page waiting to be written upon. Your thoughts drift back to your days as a teenager. You remember how many of those days were spent sitting around feeling bored because there was "nothing to do." Oh, to have just one of those Saturdays back, to trade your aches and pains for the energy, health, and opportunities you had then.

Recently we attended the funeral of our good friend's grandfather. Meredith adored her grandpa! His name was Joe Cooper. Joe was seventy-five years old, still a vibrant and physically active man when a heart attack took his life. When he was a young man, Joe had the opportunity to play professional baseball, but he walked away. It would mean too much time away from his family. The testimony shared over and over by his friends, his sons, his grandchildren, and his pastor was that Joe did not waste his years. Though their hearts were breaking, the hundreds of people at his memorial service laughed and smiled more than they cried. Joe's life was well lived.

> *You may just be killing time, but time is also killing you.*

When we eventually look back on the days we are living right now, will we be satisfied with how we spent them? Or would we trade everything for the chance to live them over again? One of life's hardest realities is this: many people have no idea how precious their life is until they've already squandered it. How many times have you said you were "just killing time" as if time is expendable? You may just be killing time, but time is also killing you. How foolish to treat life as though it is meaningless and mundane. On those basement-cleaning days we were so easily distracted, and a job that should have taken half an hour kept us down there all morning. But the silly ways we entertained ourselves paled in comparison to the fun we would have had playing outside in the fresh air once the job was done. We just didn't realize what our choices were costing us.

You only have one life to live, and nobody can live it for you. What kind of life will it be?

## One-Hit Wonders

It was a titanic battle of wills. The enemy was determined to gain another triumph. We were resolved: We would *not* go down in defeat this time! As with the many weekends before, our opponent— *boredom*—looked to once again have the upper hand. In a last-ditch

defensive effort Mike reached for the phone and everything changed
... Half an hour later ...

Flanked by comrades on the right and left, our musical instruments in hand, we took the "stage." It was our band's first gig, and we planned to make it count. This was our Woodstock, our Shea Stadium Concert, our '68 Comeback Special. Years of early morning practice and lessons culminated in this moment. A new era in music was about to begin.

Our band: Dan and Rob masterfully blowing the kazoos, Mike on lead nose-whistle, and cousin JP a crazed animal on percussion with specialization on the Tupperware dish. Our venue: outside the local grocery store. Our fans: N/A. With pitch-perfect skill, Dan introduced Beethoven's 5th Symphony in E flat. Rob joined in with ethereal polyphonic harmonies as Mike inserted a spectacular cadenza. All the while JP kept us firmly on beat with his singular solid and unbroken rhythm.

---

### COLLIDER BIO: GEORGE WHITEFIELD

As a young man, Whitefield sought to serve Christ any way he could. He became the best known preacher of his era, speaking to enormous audiences. Thousands of people were saved as a result. He began an orphanage, and his influence was a major spark for the First Great Awakening.

Many people told him to slow down his hectic schedule, but he famously declared that he would rather "burn out than rust out." As he lay on his deathbed, a crowd of people gathered in a vigil outside his house. Upon hearing they had come, Whitefield took a candle in his hand and stepped out on the balcony to preach to the crowds one last time, and when his candle finally flickered out, he went back to his bed and passed into eternity.

---

After an hour of dazzling the masses with our magnificent cacophony, we gathered the tips from our hat (75 cents) and headed inside the store to spend it on bulk candy. A musician's life is not always a glamorous one. On that historic afternoon the Cochrane Philharmonic played their first and last show.

## Pursuit of Happiness

You may think it's silly to create a ragtag band using kazoos and nose whistles, and most of the people going in and out of that grocery store would concur. But that day the four of us had a blast. Now that we are all adults and separated by thousands of miles, we share many great memories of summer days like that one where we refused to surrender to boredom.

*If you are not experiencing abundant joy, then you are living at a significantly lower level than Jesus intended for you.*

We all want joy. Ask anyone, Christian or not, what they want out of life, and "to be happy" will always come out near the top. Even the American Declaration of Independence identifies "the pursuit of happiness" as a nonnegotiable right. There's a classic scene in the movie *The Sound of Music.* Maria is the new nanny for the children of hard-nosed Captain Von Trapp. Upon arriving, she wonders about play clothes for the children, and asks the maid, "What do the children play in?" The maid replies, "The Von Trapp children don't play; they march!" The world holds a similar misconception that God is like Captain Von Trapp, a rule-imposing killjoy, and we are His children. But contrary to popular opinion, the Bible does *not* forbid people from being happy or doing fun things. In fact, God encourages it.

For example, after Jesus used the "vines and branches" metaphor to describe what the Christian life is supposed to be, He concluded, "I have spoken these things so that My joy may be in you and your joy may be complete" (John 15:11). Christians who "get it" will have His joy overflowing in their lives. The Christian life should be *defined* by joy, not devoid of it. In fact, if you are not experiencing abundant joy, then you are living at a significantly lower level than Jesus intended for you. Unfortunately, many Christians are anything but joyful. In his book *UnChristian*, David Kinnaman recalls one nonbeliever's observation of Christians in church. They are like "a pack of domestic cats that look like they are thinking deep thoughts but are just waiting for their next meal."[34]

Christians have multiple reasons to celebrate. We've been saved from sin's condemnation and brought into a personal love relationship with all-powerful God. The Holy Spirit lives in us to help us enjoy life in dimensions we didn't even know were possible. Every day is a gift. So why are we so often bored, depressed, and unfulfilled? Because we collide with a world that tells us to spend our days differently from the full life for which we were created.

## The Lie—Cave-In Response

In a generation driven by Darwinism and dominated by secular humanism, we are encouraged to create our own happiness. If the universe simply looks down on us with cold, pitiless indifference, then we must spend our few short years pursuing whatever temporal joy we can attain. However, most people are not doing a great job of making themselves happy. Read one issue of *People* magazine, and you'll see that those experiencing the most "pleasure" are usually the most miserable. German billionaire Adolf Merckle was ranked in *Forbes'* list of the top one hundred wealthy men in the world. When his financial empire began to crumble, he stepped in front of a train to end his misery. The world has its

### CULTURE CLIP: "THE BIRTHMARK"

Nathanial Hawthorne's 1846 short story tells of a happy couple, the beautiful Georgiana and her scientist husband Aylmer. Georgiana's appearance is perfect in every way. She does, however, have a small birthmark on her which she finds cute.

But to Aylmer it becomes an embodiment of imperfection. He obsesses over it, thinking that she doesn't look as she should. He eventually can't stand it anymore and invents a potion to remove the mark.

As Georgiana drinks the liquid, the mark slowly disappears! Aylmer finally has what he always wanted! However, tragically the potion also poisons her. In the end Georgiana loses the birthmark, but Aylmer loses her.

list of everything we need in order to be happy, and many people wear themselves out running after those things: perpetual youth, romance, good looks, money, stuff, more stuff, excitement, and so on. Eventually they grow exhausted by the pursuit, falling into a pit of regret when they realize the world didn't live up to its promises.

Here's a great idea for a birthday party scavenger hunt. Take the kids to the mall and set them loose in the perfume section to see who can be first to locate the following fragrance names: *Joy, Pleasure, Fulfillment, Feel Good, Euphoria,* and of course, *Happy.* They're all there, along with several others that would better suit a PG-13 party game. Most of us don't want to admit it, but we fall for the sales gimmicks. We listen to the lies of the world, and we cave in to them.

## Who Ordered the Chef Salad?

When I (Mike) was a toddler, my dad was a student, so we didn't have much money. Our luxurious seminary apartment desperately needed Ty Pennington to drop in and film an episode of *Extreme Makeover: Home Edition.* However, one object helped turn our house into a home: a pretty potted plant. It brought life and color into our little abode. But, being two years old and not very discerning, I had a nasty habit of plucking all the leaves off to make a "salad." My dad was determined to help me break that habit.

"Michael," he warned, "*do not* touch that plant. Do you understand me?" I drooled and nodded. But before I could stop myself, I reached out and grabbed a fistful of leaves. My dad quickly seized the guilty appendage and swatted it, leaving my poor little hand smarting. Although a brighter child would have learned his lesson at this point, that plant held my attention and consumed my thoughts. My personal shoulder-devil was screaming in my ear: *Touch the plant! Plant! Plant! Plant!* Immediately I reached out with my other hand and harvested it a second time. *Whack!*

This meant war. With tears welling up in my big brown eyes and my chubby little hands hanging limp and throbbing at my sides, I readied myself for one final act of rebellion. "The Man doesn't tell *me* what to do!" I turned around and backed my diaper-clad hiney into the plant. Strike Three. All that for a *salad?* Even as a winsome, adorable, cherubic, enchanting little two-year-old, I was determined to be the author of my own destiny.

## Losing Everything

Someone who had a similar experience was the first human on the planet. If ever a guy had it all, it was Adam. (For goodness sake, he got to walk around Paradise *naked*!) He lived in a lush garden, conversed with God daily, and was appointed CEO over Eden. As if that weren't enough, God created Eve for him, a perfect woman. It was like being on a dating TV show as the only contestant. But, was Adam satisfied? For a while, until Satan's trickery led him to believe he was missing something and God was holding out on the best stuff. As it happened, a plant was his downfall too, and he lost everything.

After all these millennia, the same sinful nature still tells us to risk it all for forbidden fruit. Christians live in God's presence, yet we keep sneaking out into the streets to see what we're missing. Jesus came on a rescue mission and pulled us out of our enslavement to the world, yet inevitably

### COLLIDER BIO: BRIAN "HEAD" WELCH

When Head joined the band Korn, he had no idea they would become one of the most popular rock acts in the world. The success of Korn provided everything Head had always dreamed of: money, fame, success. But something was wrong because he was completely miserable.

As substance abuse started to destroy his life, Head began a tough journey that eventually led him to faith in Christ. God completely changed him, providing everything the world had failed to deliver.

Clean from his destructive lifestyle, Head quit Korn and turned his life over to Jesus. In his autobiography he writes, "It's a full-on, risk-filled life that I believe God desires all Christians to live. It's when you completely lay down every part of your life so Christ can live through you." (Welch 2008) we straggle back toward our former bondage. What's the attraction? Why the fascination with what we don't have or need? We buy into the myth that if we had a little (or a lot) more money we'd be content. Or if we could find that drop-dead gorgeous girlfriend, the world would be our oyster. We think if we could get drunk enough, we'd find the joy that eludes us when we are sober. If a girl sleeps with the guy she idolizes, maybe then he'll cherish her the way she longs to be loved. We collide with fallacies like these every day of our lives. Most of us know they're empty promises, but we pursue them anyway.

## Lady and the Tramp(oline)

As kids we made up numerous games, along with our cousin JP. There was one we called "Raptor." It involved the three of us, a trampoline, and JP's cocker spaniel, Lady. Now, don't let the name fool you. Lady may not have been a big dog, but when she nipped at your ankles, it was enough to make a grown man cry.

The object of the game was to run around the entire house (barefoot) and make it back to the trampoline. We kept Lady on her leash, but when the runner got halfway around the house, the other two contestants would set her free. By then Lady was of course hyper from all the action. If you could reach the trampoline and leap up onto it before she caught you, you were safe. It was wintertime and the snow and ice made for a challenging and treacherous run. (Disclaimer: This was also Lady's favorite game and done playfully, not Michael Vick style.)

We all coveted the legendary featherweight "Champion of Raptor" title belt, and one day JP determined it would be his. "Go big or go home!" he boasted, daring us to do the unthinkable: send Lady mere seconds after he started running. It was pure insanity! It was utter madness! Evil Knievel would have gasped at such an outrageous stunt! It was vintage JP.

Leaping like a gazelle from the trampoline, off dashed JP. Lady was growling and pulling at her restraints. "Release the hound!" Mike bellowed, and Lady rocketed after JP, disappearing from our view.

*Seconds later . . .*

JP came slip-sliding around the other side of the house. His face was ashen, and he was running for his life! An instant later Lady hurtled into sight in hot pursuit of her prey. JP winced as Lady's jaws snapped mere millimeters from his bare ankles. In a final heroic display of determination and athleticism, our cousin launched himself through the air and onto the trampoline. He made it!

Then, as if from a horrible nightmare, Lady pounced onto a nearby pile of snow and catapulted herself up onto the trampoline. The chase resumed. Squealing like a little girl, JP bolted off the tramp

> *Jesus didn't die for us so that we could flirt with the things that sent Him to the cross in the first place.*

and hustled back around the house, with Lady nipping at his heels and the two of us laughing hysterically.

## Equally Enamored

The world offers quick, easy excitement. But the consequences of these thrills can be disastrous, even fatal. It's not that Christians don't know this fact; our problem is we play a dangerous game of trying to get as close to the line as we can without crossing it. We justify our behavior by telling ourselves, "I'll drink a beer or two; I just won't get drunk," or, "I'll get physical with my boyfriend, but I would never 'go all the way.'" When we trivialize caving in to the world, we have completely missed the point of being a Christian. Jesus didn't die for us so we could flirt with the things that sent Him to the cross in the first place. Jesus died to set us *free* from the world, not to watch us keep toying with it. The late British poet William Yeats, in his poem "The Second Coming," wrote, "Turning and turning in a widening gyre/the falcon cannot hear the falconer/ Things fall apart/the center cannot hold/mere anarchy is loosed upon the world."[35] It's a dangerous practice to inch closer and closer to the enemy because that very act takes us farther and farther from the voice of the Father.

More and more churches are buying into the notion youth events should merely be sanitized models of whatever they don't want their teenagers to be doing "out there." One youth director was wringing his hands because the teens in his church were dividing off into factions. Broken relationships and jealousy were causing rifts, mostly because of who was dating whom. So what did that youth pastor do? He scheduled a dance in the church gym, complete with chaperones, an event that put mounds of pressure on these kids to show up with a date. Should he have been surprised, then, that his youth group reflected the pressures put on them by the world? He was imitating it. We try to create Christian variations of worldly events, but if we are enamored enough to mimic the world, then we probably *are* missing out because all we are getting is a watered-down version of the real thing. Let's face it; the world does "the world" far better than Christians do, and we are foolish to try and imitate it. And besides, when we do things the world's way, we get the world's results.

> ### CULTURE CLIP: ICARUS
>
> Ancient Greek mythology tells the tale of Icarus and his father Daedalus. After enraging King Minos, the ruler of the island of Crete, the two are imprisoned within the Minotaur's labyrinth.
>
> However, Daedalus, a legendary architect of unparalleled skill, devises an escape plan. Constructing two sets of wings, the duo escapes the island by the only unguarded pathway, the air.
>
> As the island shrinks into the horizon, Icarus becomes exhilarated by the freedom of flight. Continuing to soar higher into the atmosphere, he discards his father's warning not to fly too close to the sun.
>
> But soon the heat rays from the sun melt the glue holding the wings together, and Daedalus watches his son plummet to his death.

### "I'm So Bored!"—Cave Dwellers

While Cave-Ins default to secular standards as their go-to guide for a good time, Cave Dwellers sit back and wait for the action to come to them. In North America we have the freedom to spawn every form of Christian worship style and Christian entertainment imaginable. That's great because there's a lot of diversity in the Western world so congregations can reach out to a variety of people. It's all good until Christians start to think worship styles exist to satisfy us. The fact is, worship is not primarily for us. God instituted worship as a way for *us* to honor *Him*. That means we aren't the ones to decide whether a worship service was good or bad. That's for God to judge. We once heard a worship pastor comment to his band after a set of songs, "That was some *awesome* worship!" Really? What did God think? Because it doesn't matter how much you shred on the guitar (the angels in heaven are better) since God looks at the heart. *You* may have enjoyed it, but did *God*? When we lose our focus and start to think our church must please us, we flirt with a dangerous attitude. We lose sight of the difference between worship and entertainment. Then youth pastors act more like recreation directors, and families shop around for a home church the same way they do for a leisure center. (Is there a gym? A coffee shop? A bookstore? Are the "facilities" adequate?) They join wherever they can *get* the most by *giving* the least.

Don't misunderstand what we're saying. Young people should have tons of fun, and when we were in high school and college, there was no place we'd rather be than at our church with our Christian friends. But the reason Christians have so much enjoyment should be because we have joy in our lives, not because we are well entertained. The difference is enormous.

We used to organize weekend events for our church's college gang. Depending on the activity, we could always count on the attendance to fluctuate more graphically than CD sales for the latest *American Idol* finalists. Laser tag or movie nights were guaranteed to attract the majority of the group. However, when we introduced every third week as "service week" to volunteer our time in the community, we ran up against all sorts of scheduling issues. Suddenly several people had to work, or didn't feel well, or had a family commitment, or had to study (yeah right!). Even for the more social evenings, a predictable few would always ask, "Who else will be there?" or, "What are we going to do?" The answer to those two questions determined whether they came along or stayed home. Rarely did anyone ask "How can I help make this a great event?"

It's human nature to think of what will entertain us the best and not how we can *contribute* to the joy. How often do you see a Facebook status that says, "I'm soooooo bored!" Did you know the Web site Bored.com has more than sixty thousand fans on Facebook? What we're really saying when we're constantly bored is we are unable to have joy unless someone else provides it for us. Radio host Dennis Prager bluntly observed, "'I am bored' generally means, 'I am boring.'"[36] This prevalence of boredom may be a by-product of a generation that is used to being entertained constantly, even at church. If it is not scintillating, or at least amusing, we abandon it faster than last year's outdated gaming consol. Again, it comes down to our focus. We have it backward. If Jesus has offered us abundant life and we are still spending our days bored, the problem is not with God; it is with us.

## Summary

This chapter was intended to make you think about your own life and your attitudes. If you tend to cave in and default to the world's way of keeping yourself occupied or if you're more of a Cave Dweller who sits back, bored to tears until someone else brings joy to you on a platter, please keep reading; we've saved the best for last. The next (and last) chapter will show you how to be a Collider, how to live a joyful life the way God intended, and how to share joy with others.

Joy isn't an activity or an object; it is an attitude. It's something within us that goes wherever *we* go. Jonathan Swift said, "May you *live* all the days of your life." Life is too precious to waste even one day just "killing time." If the world can't satisfy us and we can't rely on other people to give us joy, then how should we live so we have no regrets when we are older? How can we live each and every day to the max? We want to challenge you. If you are not experiencing true joy, perhaps you haven't experienced what the Christian life is all about. The world offers cheap imitations of what only God can deliver. Let's discover how to collide with that deluded way of thinking. The results may surprise you.

## SO WHAT?

1. How old are you? How have you spent the years behind you? Do you want to spend the years ahead of you *exactly the same way?* Have you thought much about reaching the end of your life? In the grand scheme of things, what is important in life? How frequently do you find yourself sitting at home with nothing to do?

2. Look at the way you have fun. In what areas have you tried to imitate the world's version of a good time? Has it been satisfying? Were you left with any regrets?

3. What's your perspective on going to church? Do you enjoy being there? Do you find it boring? If so, why? In what ways might your approach toward church create false expectations?

## WHAT NOW?

1. If you find yourself apathetic at church, take some time to think of how you can change that. Often a cure for boredom is to serve other people, and it is rewarding. Perhaps this is the week you volunteer in child care. Maybe this semester you can sign up for a worship team or join a Bible study group. Why not offer your services at the next youth or college event in whatever capacity is needed?

2. If you find yourself moping around the house with nothing to do, take a moment and pray, asking God to use you in some way. Then, instead of turning on the TV, take a walk outside and pray as you go. Amazing opportunities to help people or

share your faith will crop up when you're active to pray and look for them.

3.  Think of one way you usually entertain yourself that may not be good for you (watching edgy movies or TV shows, reading books with trashy content, listening to profanity-laced music, etc.) and replace that habit with something that honors God. This doesn't necessarily have to be reading your Bible (although that is *always* a good option), but think of another form of entertainment that either draws you closer to God or helps another person. How was this experience different from your previous entertainment choices? How did you feel afterward?

### Chapter 11

# AN INTERNAL COLLISION—
# BECOMING A PERSON OF JOY

*All the good things you love come from God,*
*but they are pleasant and good only as they*
*relate to him. Once your love deserts him,*
*things rightly turn sour, because anything from God is*
*improperly loved if it causes men to desert him.*[37]
—SAINT AUGUSTINE (EARLY CHURCH FATHER)

*The universe we observe has precisely the*
*properties we should expect if there is,*
*at bottom, no design, no purpose, no evil and*
*no good, nothing but blind, pitiless indifference.*[38]
—RICHARD DAWKINS (ATHEIST BIOLOGIST/AUTHOR)

## Egg Hunt!

A couple of years ago, I (Mike) volunteered at a local Easter Egg Hunt. The kids were sorted according to their age, and each group had ten minutes on a baseball diamond to gather as many eggs as they could. In between sets we volunteers would run around madly replenishing the supply of eggs. However, there was a slight twist. Although several thousand eggs were scattered across the field, there was one for each group worth more than the rest: The Golden Egg.

This egg contained a voucher to be cashed in for a giant basket of merchandise worth far more than the cheap treats found in the others. As one batch of kids was preparing to launch, a determined father declared, "My brother-in-law found the Golden Egg last round. This time it belongs to me and my daughter!" Sure enough, as soon as the whistle blew, this guy raced to the head of the pack. Completely ignoring the hundreds of obvious eggs, he thundered to the middle of the field, dragging his little daughter behind him. We don't know if he ever found the Golden Egg (or if the grass stains ever came out of that Easter dress), but we do know he was more determined than any other parent to come away with a worthy prize.

## Collider = Being a Person of Joy

While that dad could have used a lesson in Easter Egg Etiquette, he got one thing right. Life is too short to chase after worthless trinkets when there's a greater prize to be found. Jesus said: "The kingdom of heaven is like treasure, buried in a field, that a man found and reburied. Then in his joy he goes and sells everything he has and buys that field" (Matt. 13:44). This world has plenty of pleasures to spend our short life pursuing, and yet they are like cheap, plastic imitations compared to the life Jesus promised.

We've both enjoyed playing in worship bands for years and have been able to get a bird's-eye view of the people assembled to worship. There are usually two kinds of expressions. Some exude joy by their demeanor and their body language. You can tell they're glad to be there. Others look like they are passing a kidney stone. We had one atheist tell us, "When I see Christians, I see unhappy, complaining people. I can be unhappy *without* God."

Joy is not something we can go out and get from the outside world like we go out to grab a hamburger; nor can it be delivered to us like a pepperoni pizza. For Christians joy comes from *within*. That's because God, who *is* joy, lives *in* us. Jesus does not concern Himself with entertaining or amusing us. What He offers is so much better. It's His own Spirit, which can transform each of us into a *person* of joy. The world comes at us from the outside, but God works from the inside.

It's amazing the views people have about God. Many consider Him to be a condemning, angry supreme being, bent on restricting our fun and binding us with a long list of "thou shalt nots." But that's not the God we know, and it's certainly not the way the Gospels describe Jesus. Don't be fooled into thinking Jesus was a somber social misfit, out to restrict people's joy. Read through the Gospels and notice a reoccurring theme: Jesus attending parties. Everyone wanted Jesus at their banquets and gatherings. The sinners and tax collectors invited

> ## COLLIDER BIO: FRANCIS OF ASSISI
>
> As a young man from a wealthy family, Francis lived a carefree youth with little regard for others. He had everything he could ever ask for. However, he would discover something much deeper than the frivolous pleasures of wealth.
>
> Upon Francis's conversion his heart broke for the poor. He desperately wanted to help the impoverished masses he saw all around him so he began to share his wealth with them. His father thought him foolish, imprisoning him within the walls of their home and even beating him for giving away what he had.
>
> But Francis persisted. Eventually he renounced all his wealth and standing, even publicly stripping off the clothes on his back and handing them back to his father.
>
> Now free from the confines of worldly pursuits, Francis devoted his life to poverty and serving the poor. He developed a following that eventually became an order of monks called the Franciscans. Although he gave away everything of material value in his life, Francis gained a joy that overflowed into everything he did.

Him while the religious elite looked on from the outside scowling.

Kids loved to be around Jesus (and anyone who has ever babysat knows kids are a hard sell). Why did the party animals of that day include Jesus on their guest list? Because even the skeptics knew if He came, their party would not be dull. If you're living a dreary existence, could it be you don't really know Him? If we're bored, can we truly be following somebody who never lived a boring day in His life?

Jesus spread joy to anyone who wanted it because He had joy in abundance to give. The Irish poet Oscar Wilde once observed two different kinds of people, "Some cause happiness wherever they go; others *whenever* they go!"[39] Which one describes you? Are you living out the inextinguishable joy that comes from Christ, or are you merely putting in time? Perhaps a more telling question is: which description would your parents, girlfriend/boyfriend, schoolmates, Facebook friends, teammates, or coworkers say fits you? The previous chapter delved into how Cave-Ins and Cave Dwellers collided with life and came away joyless. Now let's see how a Collider fares.

## It's Not What or Who. . . . It's *You*

### The Dreaded Kamp Kiwanis

Kamp Kiwanis—the thin decaying clapboard walls providing only meager rations to nourish the local termites, the landscape more neglected than a prepubescent boy's deodorant stick, and the bathrooms . . . *shudder*. In contrast, a Buddhist convention was in full swing in the adjacent lot. This ghost-town campground (cue the tumbleweed) would be the site of our youth group's first retreat, although our mom almost vetoed the idea because she thought we said a *nudist* convention was going on next door.

As members of the youth leadership team, we suggested a weekend retreat. Short on planning time, our itinerary was as bare as a college student's pantry. When we passed around the sign-up sheet, an impromptu game of hot-potato broke out among the discerning youth. People couldn't get that sheet of paper out of their hands fast enough. But the appointed weekend came, and we assembled at the campsite. Only fifteen of the sixty youth were "free to come." But we—the hearty remnant—pressed on, determined it would be a good time.

As the girls were nesting in their cabin, our little band of guys threw our sleeping bags on the ground and brainstormed about fun things to do. Someone brought an old hacky sack, so we started a game of donkey. If you've never played that game, all you need to know is the loser of each round has to stand with his back to the firing squad and receive a pelting by the winners. Frustrated after losing a third straight game, our friend Jason completely snapped, throwing himself against the wall and dropping his pants. (Looks like our mom was right after all.) And the moon shone brightly in the morning sunlight.

"You guys wanna throw the sack at me again? Well, go for it!" he taunted. Suddenly a high-pitched gasp rang out. In horror, Jason looked over

---

## CULTURE CLIP: ROY HALLADAY'S PERFECT GAME

On May 29, 2010, no one expected history to be made; 43,000 empty seats remained as the last-place Florida Marlins took on division rival Philadelphia Phillies.

Phillies starting pitcher Roy Halladay took the mound and began dominating the Marlins lineup leaving a string of zeros on the scoreboard.

Bottom 9th—The crowd burst into a frenzy as Halladay retired the 27th straight hitter—pitching only the 20th perfect game in the 120-year history of Major League Baseball.

After the game, in a bizarre marketing scheme, the Marlins put for sale the remaining 43,000 empty seats at face value. To the surprise of everyone, they began to sell like crazy! Marlins president stated, "Remember, no matter how many tickets were ever bought, twenty years from now, 300,000 people will say they were there anyway."

In hindsight, many people wanted to be a part of history. However, only the handful of dedicated fans will be able to carry the historic experience with them for the rest of their lives.

his shoulder to see our youth pastor's sweet young wife. She came to get us for lunch. Her face was whiter than a Canadian blizzard. As Jason scrambled to cover himself, she called out in a shaky voice for her husband: *"Jonnnnaathannn!"* We knew we were in for a memorable weekend.

By Sunday, tales of our shenanigans and adventures had circulated around the youth group. When the Second Annual Youth Retreat rolled around, the scene was totally different. Carloads of excited teenagers poured into the campground. Everyone wanted to experience the fun this time. Who needs state-of-the-art facilities or an elaborate list of organized games when you have guys like Jason? More to the point, all you really need is a commitment to have fun regardless the circumstances.

## CULTURE CLIP: TOM SAWYER

Tom Sawyer, the famous protagonist created by novelist Mark Twain, has captured the hearts of readers for decades.

The happy-go-lucky boy is always up to some form of mischief. When given the chore of whitewashing a fence, he is determined to enjoy it.

Several of the other town boys take turns stopping by to laugh at Tom, showing off their yo-yos and captured insects and boasting about all the fun they are having.

However, Tom continues joyfully to paint the fence, turning the task into an adventure. Eventually, so intrigued by the fun Tom is experiencing, the other boys realize their trinkets aren't all that satisfying after all and they join Tom in his chore. In contrast with a jovial attitude, the toys and gadgets of the boys offered little amusement.

## Bringing the Joy with *You*

We've probably all been guilty of delaying our response to an invitation until we see who else plans to go. But why rely on other people? The common denominator for any gathering you attend is *you* are there; and if you are a joyful person, you never have to worry about whether an event will be fun. It will be a blast because *you* are there.

Say, for example, you hate bowling. Lots of people hate bowling because of the dorky shoes that hundreds of sweaty feet have already occupied. Or because the junior high girls who have laid claim to the jukebox. Or, more truthfully, because they've always stunk at bowling and they know they look like an idiot throwing gutter balls. So you get a call on a slow Friday evening; a couple of your friends want to go bowling. You can be a jerk and say, "Count me out; bowling is lame." Or you can politely decline and stay home to watch *Brady Bunch* reruns. Or, you can grab some hand sanitizer and head to the bowling alley. So you get schooled by the fifth-grade girl's birthday party in the next lane. So the manager has to demonstrate how "not to lob the ball" because you're "ruining the expensive hardwood finish." It's OK! Have some fun!

> If you are a joyful person, you never have to worry about whether an event will be fun. It will be fun because you are there.

Why do we decline to do things we think *might* not be fun when our only alternative is doing nothing? It's amazing how many people have whiled away entire evenings at home bored because they were scared they might be bored at something else. If you commit to being a fun person, then the only detail that matters is *you* are at the event.

## You Are Free in Christ so Act Stupid!

### Did I Miss the Memo?

When I (Mike) moved to North Carolina, I joined a church with a great college and young adults group. I was told the group scheduled two major events each year: The Beach Retreat and The Christmas Party. I missed the beach so I was determined to make my presence known come Christmas. To my delight, I heard it was to be a themed event. We were supposed to dress as characters from our favorite Christmas movie. After briefly wishing I had natural elf ears like Dan so I could go as a Who from Whoville, I settled on Ralphie from *A Christmas Story.* I was determined to win the prize for best costume.

Days before the event I had already excitedly assembled my costume. I found an ugly old sweater vest and tie at Goodwill as well as some thick coke-bottle glasses. The glasses were real so I couldn't see a thing with them on, but they were too perfect to pass up. To top it off, I (who only a select few have ever seen with my hair *not* spiked) slicked my hair flat to one side. In short, I looked like a kid whose mom dressed him up horribly for church. I looked like Ralphie. It was perfect.

Butterflies churned in my stomach as I got closer to the house. How many people would be there? Would I have the best costume? Would I make any new friends because of the creative genius I emitted? With a surge of confidence, I marched up the front steps and kicked open the door.

"The *Par-tay* has just arrived! Somebody toss me a Diet Coke and . . ." I froze. The room was jammed with people, and every pair of eyes was on me. No one else was dressed up.

"Hey Mike, I've never seen your hair like that!" someone called from the back of the room. I looked around, face flushed, desperately trying to find another movie character . . . a kindred spirit. I was burning up with embarrassment. But then, it was magical . . . just like in the movies. One after another, people started coming over to shake my hand or hug me. They were happy to see *me*, no matter how funny I looked. I adjusted my glasses. *Perhaps I'll win the Best Costume prize after all!*

## Free

As Christians we don't need to have all the hang-ups the world wants to throw on our shoulders. Unlike Cave-Ins, Colliders have the freedom to enjoy life without the pressure to "fit in" or be like everybody else—the freedom to look like an absolute geek at a costume party. We know who we are. We've been bought with a high price, and we are free. True joy comes from freedom.

When we were growing up, our house was the center for some bizarre parties. Most of them involved costumes, and more often than not, Dan was a girl. His best was probably Pocohontas, but Britney Spears was a runner-up. It became second nature for us to throw a costume together. In fact, we collected costumes and props. The closet in our guest room looked like a costume cabinet at Universal Studios. We only had two Golden Rules if you wanted to come: (1) You *had* to wear a costume, or we reserved the right to dress you in one at the door; and (2) You had to have a good attitude.

Dan's wife Sarah met a girl who grew up in the same neighborhood we did, so she began to describe our house. The girl instantly recognized it, "Oh, you mean the house that always has the crazy parties!" Christians, at least in the eyes of that young unbeliever, were anything but boring.

### A 9.5 for Style

The hockey rink—a blissful oasis of joyful memories where magical moments happen more frequently than at Hogwarts. A haven of nostalgia—a place where friendships are born and battles are won, and for some a place where we hopelessly attempt to recapture our pre-twenty-college-pound glory.

Steven Spielberg couldn't have scripted it any more dramatically. Rallying from a two-goal deficit, my (Dan) team forced overtime in remarkable fashion. The extra session solved nothing, so the game hinged on the most exciting moment in hockey—the shootout. Back and forth it went, with neither team able to claim the upper hand. Eventually all sixteen players on both teams tried their luck on the opposing goalie . . . except for me.

Adding to the storybook tilt was Sarah had never seen me play. She was visiting from Canada and two days earlier became my fiancée. As I took center ice, the fate of the game resting on my stick, I winked to her, "After the killer moves I'm about to make, you'll never regret signing on to my team for life."

Rocketing forward with superhuman speed, I gathered up the puck and vaulted down the ice. In the next millisecond I gauged the goalie was weak glove-side, would be fooled by my triple-deke, and was of west-Ukrainian descent. Spurred on by the infatuated cheers of my fiancée, I launched a complex pattern of precision moves with my stick, some too quick to be seen by the naked eye, then . . . *whoosh!*

In a blur of motion I realized my skates were pointing heavenward and I was hurling through the air at approximately twenty miles an hour. My skate caught an edge.

Pirouetting across the sky, my body executed a series of triple salchows and double lutzes not seen since Kristi Yamaguchi's prime. Bouncing off the ice's surface, I completed a beautiful double-single-double combination. With a flurry of climactic motion—*bang!*—I slammed into the boards. It's a tough call which was more humiliating, limping into the dressing room to face the guys or trying to convince Sarah not to give the ring back.

Real life doesn't always play out like it does in the movies. Instead of winning one for the team and being hoisted onto my teammates' shoulders as they sang "We Are the Champions," I spent the next hour spitting out ice chips and wishing Sarah could get herself together and stop laughing.

Only one thing would have been worse than what happened, and that was not ever getting to play the game at all. Don't ever let fear of losing or looking stupid hold you back from enjoying life. Your tombstone isn't going to have your impressive Monopoly win/loss ratio on it. If your friends or youth group are playing a game and you don't understand the rules, join in and learn as you go. If they're singing karaoke and you can't carry a tune in a bucket, get up and let your off-pitch vocals fly. No one remembers the winner, but nobody forgets the laughter they shared while playing. Don't let self-consciousness hold you back. Experience the joy of Christ.

## Don't Just Sit There . . . Do Something

### Bored Much?

Facebook came out with an application to rank the top ten words appearing most often in a person's status. The results were sometimes predictable (such as our sister's most frequent words, i.e., *shop, buy, mall, Prada*), but no doubt lots of people were surprised by what came up. What would your words be? If *bored* is on that list, it's time to do something about that. Don't sit around waiting for someone to invite you out. Get something started.

Jared was well liked and respected by the other youth at our church, but he was kind of quiet so people didn't always think to call him when they were having a get-together. However, he was determined to have fun regardless whether he received a social invitation every weekend. He'd gather some of the other guys who weren't busy, and they'd work out together or do something smart like make a robot (they were all brilliant). These guys didn't just *go* to a movie; they would *make* a movie, complete with special effects. They were having a blast every weekend, and they taught us a valuable lesson: most of the time when nothing is happening it's because everyone is waiting for someone else to make the first move.

When *American Idol* was in its heyday, it conveniently came on right after our church's midweek meeting. We started inviting whoever was into the show to come over and watch it with us. After a few weeks even those who weren't fans came along because they wanted to be a part of things. There was no sign-up sheet for snacks, but someone always brought something good. By the evening of the finale, we had forty people in our living room to watch it. It was never an exclusive event; anyone was welcome. Several regulars usually wore their pajamas. The great thing about being in a youth group is you're bonded by something much deeper than the latest clique: the blood of Christ. You are family. Church should be the last place where people are labeled "cool" and "uncool," and the years of youth group can make for some of the most joyful memories of your life.

The world will tell you you're not cool unless the popular kids invite you to their parties. You could have countless invitations from other people to hang out, but if you don't get an invite to Joe Cool's house Friday night, then you must be a loser. Well, what if Joe Cool isn't as awesome as he thinks he is? What if Miss Popular is actually all hype? It's sometimes a shock for the "Really Big Deal" kids when they go on to college or work and they suddenly find out how little their popularity matters postgraduation. Suddenly no one is all that interested in every touchdown they made at Podunk High. Popularity is as fickle as the weather. Don't sweat it if you feel like you're on the periphery of the crowd "everyone" wants to be in. That's the world telling you what it takes to be cool. Collide with that way of thinking, and make whatever crowd *you* swing in the cool crowd.

## Hang On to Your Joy

### Birthday Boys Are So Last Year

It was a birthday party of unprecedented magnificence. Marie Antoinette would have blushed from its audacious extravagance. The decorations were stupendous. And the food . . . mounds of savory cookies stacked in columns like coins and lush cakes with gluttonous lumps of icing oozing down their chocolaty sides. Over in the corner, I (Dan) spied a hoard of goodie bags, brimming over like Santa's toy sack. The party was perfect in every way. All that was lacking was the birthday boy.

The evening commenced like most ten-year-old boys' birthday parties, the compact room dense with giggling girls and the paralyzing stench of active boys who neglected to shower. To kick off the celebration, we gathered around the game table. Then it happened.

Having lost game one, the birthday boy hurled the table aside, screaming and launching out venomous accusations at all the "cheaters" who had bested him. This unfortunate spectacle proceeded for several tense minutes before his mother bellowed thunderously over the crowd, "Kevin, you are grounded!" The awkward-O-meter shot way up. We stood in silence as the guilty culprit was escorted, still wailing, to his room. When his mother reappeared, alone, she nonchalantly asked, "All right then, who's ready for cake?"

For the next hour the rest of us partied to our hearts' content. We chased down the cake with double chocolate chunk ice cream. I made it to the finals in musical chairs but was not as lucky in pin the tail on the donkey. The movie ran a little long, cutting into the scheduled gift-opening time, but as luck would have it, the intended recipient was still in solitary confinement upstairs. We had just completed the treasure hunt when the parents arrived. All in all, it was a fantastic party. When I finally saw Kevin three days later at school, I patted him on the back, "*Great* party, man. We should do it again sometime!"

## Little Thieves

We miss out on a joyful life when we allow trivial matters to steal our joy. Jesus is the joy giver, and the Bible says no one can take His joy away from us (John 16:22). The only way to lose our joy is to surrender it voluntarily.

What sorts of things ruin your day? If a rude driver honks at you on the freeway or the McDonalds cashier is snarly, do you fume about it for the rest of the day? Insignificant annoyances that consume our thoughts and fuel our rants are not worth the time we waste over them.

## Drawing from the Well

Several years ago I (Mike) traveled to Qatar with my father. We entered the gated community and were met by guards carrying giant guns. One of them broke off from the others and started marching toward us. *Oh, no*, I thought, *we just broke some obscure Middle Eastern law!* However, the man grinned broadly as he leaned into the driver's-side window. "Welcome, my friends!" He looked to the backseat: "You must be Mike! My name is James!" He greeted us with a radiant smile all week every time we came or went from the complex.

That week was a flurry of activity. I met fascinating people, led Bible studies, ate sheep brains (*which did NOT taste like chicken*), and even got to drive a quad through sand dunes overlooking the Persian Gulf. The day we left, James dropped in to say good-bye. That's when I learned his story.

James was originally from Sudan, Africa, where he suffered persecution for his Christianity. He was forced from his home and his job and eventually found work in Qatar. He sent his small wages home to his wife and children whom he had to leave behind in the Sudan. He was allowed to return home once every two years to see them. James worked twelve hours a day, seven days a week, trying to earn enough money to bring his family to join him. He bunked in a small concrete room with three other men. He owned nothing. His coworkers regularly mocked him for his Christian faith and taunted him about his situation. At one point a man offered James more money than he could make in a year if he would renounce Christ and adopt a different religion. James refused. The last thing he said to us, with a smile on his face, was, "But I'm a Christian, and no one can take that from me!"

Isaiah 12:3 says, "You will joyfully draw water from the springs of salvation." James understood joy. Do we? Have we lost the wonder of our salvation? That same well, which is the love of Christ, offers us an abundance of water, yet many of us are needlessly parched with thirst.

## Be a Mandy

### Mandy

Everyone needs a Mandy. I (Dan) met her during her junior year of college and was instantly intrigued by her. She had one of the softest spirits and most sacrificial hearts I ever encountered. She was always on the lookout for how to encourage others around her. When she realized many of the commuting students were eating their lunches alone in their cars, she helped organize a luncheon every Thursday to provide them with free hot food and a place to meet together, even though she was not a commuter herself. For Mandy, joy was not just about her. God was using her to spread waves of joy across campus.

> We often think of joy in terms of getting and not what we can give others.

There aren't enough Mandys in the world. It's much more natural for us to receive than to give. We often think of joy in terms of *getting* and not what we can give others. Jesus said it's better to give than to receive (Acts 20:35). We love to be blessed by God but are often disinterested in being a blessing to others. But it's amazing how far a few encouraging words can go to brighten up somebody's day.

### Spread It Around

One of Christianity's many paradoxes is that being unselfish is actually more rewarding than being selfish. This definitely collides with a world that says, "It's all about *me!*" When we take our eyes off ourselves, it's amazing how many of the little joy-stealers we no longer notice. When joy is not about us, it becomes much harder to lose. It's also limitless. Do you and your friends have a free evening? Why not drop in to a local nursing home and do a puzzle with a lonely senior? Or kidnap someone in your youth group who's often

> One of the greatest cures for boredom is spreading joy to others.

on the outskirts and go for pizza? Or rake leaves in your neighbor's yard or shovel the snow from their driveway. One of the best pick-me-ups is spreading joy to others.

### A Guest that Gives

It's human nature to take rather than to give. Every youth or college group has lifesavers and leeches. By this stage in the book you know who cousin JP is. Well, JP is a lifesaver. He's always up for whatever the event, whether it's a silly game or a workday painting someone's house or helping them move. He's the one who stops by the store and picks up some wings, soda, or whatever we need. He laughs easily and will wear any costume you hand him. He has

> A selfless guest is a frequent guest.

saved many parties from being duds, just by being himself. Then there are the leeches. They complain about everything. Nothing is cool enough, tasty enough, or fun enough for their standards. And they wouldn't be caught dead helping clean up. Who would you rather be around?

Colliders are selfless. Here's a hint we've learned over the years: want to know how to be at the top of every party's guest list? Become a guest who gives. It's as easy as that. Here are six simple rules to follow to be a party guest who is always invited back:

1. Offer to come early and help set up (but if you're not going to help, *don't* come early).
2. Always bring food or offer to chip in for the groceries (or gas if the event involves driving).
3. Don't sit back waiting to be entertained; suggest a game or see what you can do to help.
4. Don't hog the limelight. There's no worse party repellent than an attention-seeking bore.
5. Stay and help clean up (if you don't know what to do, ask).
6. Thank the hosts for all their efforts.

Acting unselfishly has a way of rewarding itself. A selfless guest is a frequent guest. If you are the kind of guest who gives, good for you. If not, don't blame your host if the party is miserable; the mood may pick up after you go home.

## Be Creative!

### Clones

Mike spent one summer working for The Town (a.k.a. The Man) doing landscaping. Monday mornings always brought the same conversation among his coworkers. One of them got "totally hammered" over the weekend, another was "completely smashed," while a third was "absolutely trashed," and so on. They were continually searching for new ways of saying, "I spent the weekend drunk."

It's funny, for a world that accuses Christians of being party poopers, too sheltered to have a good time, these people weren't doing much to present an attractive alternative. Why is it those who mock Christians for being narrow-minded are the same ones who flock like sheep to the same bars every weekend with the same people to do the same thing everyone else has been doing every weekend? Not exactly following in Galileo's footsteps. Mike's coworkers moved up to getting more drunk when getting drunk still left them empty. Now *that's* a good time. OK, maybe not.

The world's portrayal of fun leaves little room to be flexible. Every weekend Facebook sports albums of the parties that went down. Every album looks the same: the girls dressed to kill and the boys acting crazy with a bottle of beer in hand, either dancing at a club or slumped on someone's couch, eyes rolled back in their heads. Dan once had a friend tell him, "I just can't be happy anymore unless I'm drunk." Is this really the pinnacle of happiness? On the contrary. A young man from Mexico moved to our town and immediately found the party scene. To him a good time meant getting drunk enough to fight anyone who mocked his poor English. Then he met a Latino man from our church through a drop-in soccer league and was introduced to Jesus. When he got baptized, he explained how easy it was to quit drinking. "I didn't need to drink anymore; I had something better. I finally had a *reason* to give up the party scene." Wow, if only our generation could grasp this simple truth. Kids from Christian homes seem to have an especially hard time declining the world's advances. They think they're somehow missing out on all the activities forbidden to them their whole lives. That's why many of them go AWOL in college. They're finally free to indulge in the world's offerings. But talk to those who lived in the world before they knew Christ, and they'll tell you a different story. To them Jesus provided a reason to leave the shallow pleasures of the world behind.

> Nothing could be more wretched than to be intolerably depressed as soon as one is reduced to introspection with no means of diversion. —Blaise Pascal

### Unusual

Growing up, we loved to try and think outside the box whenever we got together with our friends. Several times we came up with crazy costumes and filmed hilarious improv movies with a handheld camera. One Halloween when we were teenagers, a bunch of us guys tried reverse trick-or-treating. We squeezed ourselves into our sister's little dress-up clothes and went door to door handing *in* treats. People loved us (we were awfully cute in those little dresses) and showered us with candy bars and chips. It was a stroke of brilliance. Some evenings we simply made a campfire and grabbed a guitar. Or we'd pull mattresses out into the yard, lie under the stars, and talk about stuff that mattered to us. (A word of advice though, be sure to clear out before your sprinkler system kicks on.) Often the best memories are made without ever spending a dime.

It doesn't take a huge IQ to see how much beer you can drink or how many movies you can fit in during a weekend. What do you do with your friends when you're bored? We're not trying to tell you to do the same things we did. The point is, there are endless amounts of things to do, and we want to challenge you: don't fall into a funk and one day realize you spent your entire youth living the same weekend over and over. Find your joy in God, and learn to spread that joy around. Not only will you become a cheerful person, but so will those around you.

## Summary

Life is extremely precious. Every minute spent is a minute we'll never get back. Jesus left us with a perfect model of how to live to the fullest. His life was radical, unpredictable, revolutionary, exciting, and daring—anything but boring. Author Henry David Thoreau stated, "I wished to live deliberately . . . and not, when I came to die, discover that I had not lived . . . I wanted to live deep and suck out all the marrow of life."[40]

The amount of joy we experience in our life is nobody's responsibility but our own. There's no need to live a boring life. Let's collide with the way the world views a good time, and let's do it with a smile on our faces!

## SO WHAT?

1. How often do you get bored? What's the usual cause? How do you respond when that happens?
2. What are some positive things you could do the next time boredom begins to set in? What are some different alternatives from what you normally do?
3. Are you someone who waits for things to happen, or do you *make* things happen? If you usually rely on others to entertain you, what's one way you could show some initiative this week to plan something fun? What could you do that includes or encourages someone else?

## WHAT NOW?

1. This weekend do something different from your usual routine. Make an epic movie with your friends. (Include costumes and at least one battle scene!) Invent a new game or make a twist on an old one. Do a scavenger hunt at the mall or around your neighborhood that gets total strangers involved. Be creative and have fun.
2. The next time you hang out with your friends or go to a party, put into practice the things we've mentioned about being a good houseguest. Note what happens. Did the mood change? Did anyone thank you? How did you feel afterward?
3. When your fellow students or coworkers start droning on about their latest drunk-fest, shake up the conversation by telling them what you did (after completing #1, of course) and see what happens. They may think you're weird, but hey, you may also spark their curiosity.

# CONCLUSION

## All the Colors of the Hair?

It was 2002 and I (Mike) was in eleventh grade. My high school and junior high years had been an unpredictable road, including several unpleasant twists and turns as I tried to "find myself." My journey to express the real me called for a few changes: I traded in my clarinet for a set of drums, I replaced my mushroom haircut with a trendier look, I started buying jeans instead of sweatpants, and I swapped my Star Wars books for . . . uh . . . harder-to-read Star Wars books. But as I neared the end of high school, it seemed time for a little more aggressive image management. That's when I got an idea . . . an awful idea . . . a brilliantly awful idea . . . I would dye my hair. With a drastically altered appearance I was *sure* to get noticed.

Not just any careless moderation of the tresses would do. I needed something radical. The stylist worked her magic, and when she spun my chair around, I gazed at the extravagant masterpiece she fashioned. The sides and back were my natural brown, the top was bleached blonde, and a tuft in front was fire-engine red. It was perfect!

Ecstatic, I pranced out of the dimly lit studio into the afternoon sun, ready for the world to witness the new me. The brighter light brought a shocking realization. That tuft was not so much red as pink! *I had pink hair!* Horrors! I had to face my classmates in less than fifteen hours. In desperation I called my cousin Anita and begged for help. She cleaned the local drugstore out of hair-dye kits and came rushing to my rescue. After five attempts to strip the color, the pink atrocity remained vibrant as ever. To make matters worse, somehow word made it to my school before I did. I was quickly dubbed "Mike Pinkaby." Well, at least I got noticed.

## Standing Out

Do people notice anything different about Christians? Do we stand out at all, and if so, is it positive recognition? We're about to conclude this journey with you. Thanks for allowing us to share crazy stories and some personal struggles. It's all been for one purpose, hoping you'll be challenged to collide with the world and impact our generation.

We've talked a lot about stepping up and standing out; being different in a world that has rejected God. But hopefully you've understood the challenge is not to stand out *just to be* different. There are all sorts of selfish motivations in wanting to get noticed. But Matthew 5:16 says, "Let your light shine before men, so that they may see your good works and give glory to your Father in heaven." When people look at you, they should see Jesus. Even if it takes awhile for them to discern what you're all about, your life should be a consistent message to them that the world's way isn't the only available choice. So much hurt, depression, loneliness, confusion, apathy, and anger are circulating through our generation, passed from one empty life to another. So many destructive, dangerous, and downright foolish decisions are made every day because people don't realize they have the choice of freedom. Colliders don't want people to notice *them*; they want people to see God. This world has turned away from God, and Jesus wants to use us to draw them back.

Don't be afraid to stand up, for we have been called to do so by God Himself, and He will be our guide and our strength to do everything He has asked of us. The great preacher Charles Spurgeon once said, "If sinners be damned, at least let them leap to hell over our bodies. And if they will perish, let them perish with our arms around about their knees, imploring them to stay. If hell must be filled, at least let it be filled in the teeth of our exertions, and let no one go there unwarned and unprayed for."[41]

## Running Club Inc.

I (Dan) am not exactly renowned for making health-conscious choices. This character flaw traces back to my childhood. As babies, my brother and sister crawled; I rolled. Perhaps this was due to my cheeks, which served as anchors. My globular physique carried into teenage years due to a growing addiction. When I was cut, I bled McDonald's grease. After surpassing yet another milestone in weight, I knew it was time for change. It was time for Running Club Inc.

As club president and founder, I vowed the evil forces of calories would no longer run rampant throughout my body unchecked. My club's motto was simple: *Calories don't take days off, and neither should we.*

I designed the official Web site and commenced recruiting. I quickly drafted my sister Carrie and offered her the lucrative position of vice-president and special events coordinator. With my executive team in place, we invited the masses to apply for available spots in the club.

With our ambitious publicity campaign leaping into action, we intended Running Club Inc. to be as popular as Facebook. Upon the closure of our marketing blitz, we conducted a roll call. Including Carrie and me, our prestigious Club's membership now boasted a total of . . . two. Realizing that perhaps people were hesitant to join a club whose poster boy looked like Jabba the Hutt, I made an executive decision; the show must go on.

We made the trek to a running store where they fit us with scientifically designed, state-of-the-art running shoes Usain Bolt would envy, high-quality running socks featuring advanced breathing technology, along with custom-fit headbands, and indestructible water bottles. With such cutting-edge equipment I began seriously to consider making a bid for the summer Olympic team.

To celebrate our progress we planned the Club kick-off party. We'd open with icebreaker activities, transitioning into a meet-and-greet, and end by planning an itinerary while enjoying some low-carb snacks.

A few weeks later during dinner, my dad inquired about our club's progress. Being the respected and esteemed club president, I stood and gave a detailed report, putting emphasis on the great success of our kickoff party. Obviously impressed, he posed a troubling question, "That's great. How's the running?"

"Dad, do you have *any* idea how much work goes into administering a club like this!? With all this paperwork, press conferences, and executive duties to perform, how can you expect me to fit time in to run? Now if you'll excuse me, I have a long-range planning meeting in five."

## Stepping Up

We sincerely pray you don't treat colliding the same way Dan approached Running Club Inc. You've hopefully been challenged, but challenges never translated into action are a waste of time. It's easy to be inspired today by all the Christian books, songs, and seminars out there. Most Christians know exactly what God wants them to do; they just aren't doing it. We hope you enjoyed reading this book, but more than that we hope it pushed you to become a Collider. In his book *The Power Through Prayer*, E. M. Bounds wrote, "Men are God's method. The church is looking for better methods; God is looking for better men."[42] How will God choose to change our generation? Through *us!* We don't need a great marketing strategy to demonstrate the power of Christ; we need to *live* it. Chuck Colson wrote, "If our culture is to be transformed, it will happen from the bottom up—from ordinary believers practicing apologetics over the backyard fence or around the barbecue grill."[43]

## One Day at a Time

A framed picture at our parents' house shows our grandpa, Henry Blackaby, in the East Room of the White House. He is shaking the hand of President George W. Bush Jr. Our grandpa has preached and taught in more than one hundred countries. He has spoken before world leaders at the United Nations, has met with four U.S. presidents, preached at the Pentagon, met several world leaders, and mentored Christian CEOs of Fortune 500 companies. God has used his life to make an impact all over the world for Christ. Before all that, twenty years ago, he was asked to write a little study course for our denomination *Experiencing God,* to be used in local churches. It was about how he learned to watch for where God is at work and join Him. That simple message caught on and has sold more than seven million copies and been translated into more than fifty languages. But guess what? Our grandpa is a pretty ordinary guy. As a boy he surrendered his life to Christ and made a simple but earnest commitment to live each day obeying whatever God told him to do. Now, seven decades later, his life is the result of that decision, and his commitment is to *stick with it.*

When you put this book down, we hope you'll immediately start going against the voices of the world. Following Christ into the collisions of life will be the most rewarding thing you ever do. So let's get out there and watch in amazement as God changes our generation through our lives . . . when worlds collide.

# NOTES

1. Sam S. Rainer III, "Going, Going, But Not Forever Gone?" in *HomeLife*, February 2009, 62.

2. Chuck Colson, *How Now Shall We Live?* (Wheaton, IL: Tyndale House, 1999), 13.

3. Friedrich Nietzsche, *The Gay Science*, trans. Walter Kaufman (New York: Penguin, 1974), 57.

4. Sam Harris, *Letter to a Christian Nation* (New York: Vintage Books, 2008), 4.

5. Vincent Van Gogh, the Quotations Page, http://www.quotationspage.com/quote/36359.html (accessed June 21, 2010).

6. R. C. Sproul, *Pleasing God* (Wheaton, IL: Tyndale House Publishers, reissue edition, 1994), 150.

7. Jonathan Edwards, *The Religious Affections* (Carlise, PA: Banner of Truth Trust, 2007), 316.

8. Bertrand Russell, *Why I Am Not a Christian and Other Essays on Religion and Related Subjects* (New York: Simon & Schuster, 1957), 14.

9. David Kinnaman, *UnChristian* (Grand Rapids, MI: Baker Books, 2007), 48.

10. John R. Stott, *The Cross of Christ* (Downers Grove: IVP Books, 2006), 250.

11. Russell, *Why I Am Not a Christian*, 25.

12. Jean Edward Smith, *Grant* (New York: Touchstone, 2001), 403.

13. Jung Chang and Jon Halliday, *Mao: The Unknown Story* (New York: Alfred A. Kopf, 2005), 49–50.

14. Dietrich Bonhoeffer, *The Cost of Discipleship* (New York: Touchstone, 1995), 59.

15. C. S. Lewis, *The Screwtape Letters* (New York: HarperSanFransico, 1996), 163.

16. Christopher Hitchens, *God Is Not Great: How Religion Poisons Everything* (New York: Twelve, 2007), 64.

17. Cited from http://www.martin-niemoeller-stiftung.de/4/daszitat (accessed June 22, 2010).

18. C. S. Lewis, *The Problem of Pain* (New York: HarperSanFransisco, 1996), 91.

19. Harris, *Letter to a Christian Nation,* 55.

20. Charles Dickens, *Great Expectations* (London: Penguin, 1963), 520–21.

21. Check it out at www.flight36.org.

22. Dick Staub, *The Cultural Savvy Christian* (San Francisco, CA: John Wiley & Son, 2007), 101.

23. Neil Postman, *Amusing Ourselves to Death: Public Discourse in the Age of Show Business* (New York: Penguin, 1985), 92.

24. David Platt, *Radical: Taking Back Your Faith from the American Dream* (Colorado Springs, CO: Multnomah, 2010), 7.

25. Michael Meved, *Hollywood vs. America: Popular Culture and the War on Traditional Values* (New York: HarperCollins, 1992), 115.

26. T. M. Moore, *Redeeming Popular Culture: A Kingdom Approach* (Phillipsburg, NJ: P&R, 2003), 39.

27. Hugh Heffner, cited in Rita Cosby, "Hugh Hefner on Fifty Years of *Playboy*," FOX News (September 20, 2003).

28. Johnny Cash, *Johnny Cash: The Autobiography* (New York: HarperPaperbacks, 1997), 306.

29. Josh Rottenberg, "Movie, Money & God," *Entertainment Weekly*, May 15, 2009, 28–33.

30. C. S. Lewis, *God in the Dock: Essays on Theology and Ethics* (Grand Rapids, MI: Eerdmans Publishing Company, 1970), 93.

31. C. S. Lewis in Wayne Martindale and Jerry Root, eds., *The Quotable Lewis* (Carol Stream, IL: Tyndale House Publishers, 1990), 352.

32. Ernest Hemmingway, *Quotations*, About.com, http://quotations.about.com/od/morepeople/a/hemingwayquotes.htm (accessed June 21, 2010).

33. Ernest Hemmingway, *Quotations Book*, http://quotationsbook.com/quote/23667 (accessed June 21, 2010).

34. David Kinnaman, *UnChristian* (Grand Rapids, MI: Baker Books, 2007), 122.

35. William Butler Yeats. "The Second Coming" In *The Longman Anthology of British Literature* 4th ed., ed. by David Damrosch and Kevin J. H. Dettmar (Boston, MA:Pearson Education, 2010), 2183.

36. Dennis Prager, *Thinkexist.com*, http://en.thinkexist.com/quotes/Dennis_Prager (accessed June 21, 2010).

37. Sherwood E. Wirt, *The Confessions of Saint Augustine in Modern English* (Grand Rapids, MI: Zondervan, 1981), 61.

38. Richard Dawkins, *River Out of Eden: A Darwinian View of Life* (London: Phoenix, 1995), 133.

39. Oscar Wilde, *The Quotations Page*, http://www.quotationspage.com/quote/36453.html (accessed June 21, 2010).

40. Henry David Thoreau, "Walden" in *The Norton Anthology of American Literature, vol. B*, ed. Nina Baym (New York: Norton, 2007).

41. See http://www.biblebb.com/files/spurgeon/0349.htm.

42. See http://www.leaderu.com/cyber/books/bounds/power.html.

43. Charles Colson and Nancy Pearcey, *How Now Shall We Live?* (Wheaton, IL: Tyndale House Publishers, 1999), 32.

# EXPANDED SCRIPTURE TAKEN FROM THE HOLMAN CHRISTIAN STANDARD BIBLE

### Chapter 1

**Ephesians 6:12:** "For our battle is not against flesh and blood, but against the rulers, against the authorities, against the world powers of this darkness, against the spiritual forces of evil in the heavens."

**John 5:24:** "I assure you: Anyone who hears My word and believes Him who sent Me has eternal life and will not come under judgment but has passed from death to life."

**Matthew 25:41:** "Then He will also say to those on the left, 'Depart from Me, you who are cursed, into the eternal fire prepared for the Devil and his angels!'"

**Ephesians 2:2:** "In which you previously walked according to this worldly age, according to the ruler of the atmospheric domain, the spirit that is now working in the disobedient."

**1 Corinthians 10:31:** "Therefore, whatever you eat or drink, or whatever you do, do everything for God's glory."

**Philippians 4:8:** "Finally, brothers, whatever is true, whatever is honorable, whatever is just, whatever is pure, whatever is lovely, whatever is commendable—if there is any moral excellence and if there is any praise—dwell on these things."

**John 10:10:** "A thief comes only to steal and to kill and to destroy. I have come that they may have life and have it in abundance."

### Chapter 2

None

### Chapter 3

**Matthew 5:13–16:** "You are the salt of the earth. But if the salt should lose its taste, how can it be made salty? It's no longer good for anything but to be thrown out and trampled on by men. You are the light of the world. A city situated on a hill cannot be hidden. No one lights a lamp and puts it under a basket, but rather on a lamp stand, and it gives light for all who are in the house. In the same way, let your light shine before men, so that they may see your good works and give glory to your Father in heaven."

**Luke 19:10:** "For the Son of Man has come to seek and to save the lost."

**John 17:18:** "As You sent Me into the world, I have also sent them into the world."

### Chapter 4

**Matthew 25:21:** "His master said to him, 'Well done, good and faithful slave! You were faithful over a few things; I will put you in charge of many things. Share your master's joy!'"

**1 Peter 5:8:** "Be sober! Be on the alert! Your adversary the Devil is prowling around like a roaring lion, looking for anyone he can devour."

**Matthew 28:19–20:** "Go, therefore, and make disciples of all nations, baptizing them in the name of the Father and of the Son and of the Holy Spirit, teaching them to observe everything I have commanded you. And remember, I am with you always, to the end of the age."

**2 Chronicles 34:3:** "In the eighth year of his reign, while he was still a youth, Josiah began to seek the God of his ancestor David, and in the twelfth year he began to cleanse Judah and Jerusalem of the high places, the Asherah poles, the carved images, and the cast images."

**1 Timothy 4:12:** "No one should despise your youth; instead, you should be an example to the believers in speech, in conduct, in love, in faith, in purity."

**Philippians 2:20–22:** "For I have no one else like-minded who will genuinely care about your interests; all seek their own interests, not those of Jesus Christ. But you know his proven character, because he has served with me in the gospel ministry like a son with a father."

**Ephesians 6:10–11:** "Finally, be strengthened by the Lord and by His vast strength. Put on the full armor of God so that you can stand against the tactics of the Devil."

**Ecclesiastes 12:14:** "For God will bring every act to judgment, including every hidden thing, whether good or evil."

**James 2:19:** "You believe that God is one; you do well. The demons also believe—and they shudder."

### Chapter 5

**Matthew 28:20:** "And remember, I am with you always, to the end of the age."

**Hebrews 13:5:** "I will never leave you or forsake you."

**Matthew 16:24:** "Then Jesus said to His disciples, 'If anyone wants to come with Me, he must deny himself, take up his cross, and follow Me."

**Luke 6:46:** "Why do you call me 'Lord, Lord,' and don't do the things I say?"

**Mark 1:17:** "'Follow Me,' Jesus told them, 'and I will make you fish for people!'"

### Chapter 6

**John 10:10:** "A thief comes only to steal and to kill and to destroy. I have come that they may have life and have it in abundance."

**Luke 1:37:** "For nothing will be impossible with God."

### Chapter 7

**James 4:8:** "Draw near to God, and He will draw near to you."

**Matthew 11:28–30:** "Come to Me, all of you who are weary and burdened, and I will give you rest. All of you, take up My yoke and learn from Me, because I am gentle and humble in heart, and you will find rest for yourselves. For My yoke is easy and My burden is light."

**Joshua 1:5:** "No one will be able to stand against you as long as you live. I will be with you, just as I was with Moses. I will not leave you or forsake you."

**John 16:22** "So you also have sorrow now. But I will see you again. Your hearts will rejoice, and no one will rob you of your joy."

**Acts 16:25:** "About midnight Paul and Silas were praying and singing hymns to God, and the prisoners were listening to them."

### Chapter 8

**John 17:18:** "As You sent Me into the world, I have also sent them into the world."

**2 Corinthians 5:20:** "Therefore, we are ambassadors for Christ; certain that God is appealing through us, we plead on Christ's behalf, 'Be reconciled to God.'"

**Matthew 10:16:** "Look, I am sending you out like sheep among wolves. Therefore be as shrewd as serpents and as harmless as doves."

**Matthew 15:16–19:** "'Are even you still lacking in understanding?' He asked. 'Don't you realize that whatever goes into the mouth passes into the stomach and is eliminated? But what comes out of the mouth comes from the heart, and this defiles a man. For from the heart come evil thoughts, murders, adulteries, sexual immoralities, thefts, false testimonies, blasphemies."

### Chapter 9

**Matthew 6:19:** "Don't collect for yourselves treasures on earth, where moth and rust destroy and where thieves break in and steal."

**Romans 12:2:** "Do not be conformed to this age, but be transformed by the renewing of your mind, so that you may discern what is the good, pleasing, and perfect will of God."

**1 Peter 1:14–15:** "As obedient children, do not be conformed to the desires of your former ignorance but, as the One who called you is holy, you also are to be holy in all your conduct; for it is written, Be holy, because I am holy."

### Chapter 10

None

### Chapter 11

**Acts 20:35:** "In every way I've shown you that by laboring like this, it is necessary to help the weak and to keep in mind the words of the Lord Jesus, for He said, 'It is more blessed to give than to receive.'"

# ABOUT THE AUTHORS

## Mike Blackaby

Mike is the minister to college and young adults at First Baptist Church, Jonesboro, Georgia. He grew up in Canada where he earned a BA degree at Ambrose University, Calgary, Alberta. He graduated in 2010 with a master of divinity from Southeastern Baptist Theological Seminary in North Carolina. Mike is the eldest son of Richard and Lisa Blackaby and the eldest grandchild of Henry and Marilynn Blackaby. He has traveled across North America and to several other countries, including Qatar, South Africa, Botswana, Singapore, and Malaysia speaking to young adults on the Christian life. Mike is a musician, and he has enjoyed playing drums and guitar in numerous bands. He loves hot dogs and *hates* spiders!

## Daniel Blackaby

Daniel is a student at Golden Gate Baptist Theological Seminary in San Francisco. He grew up in Canada where he developed a love for hockey. Daniel earned a BA degree in English from North Greenville University in South Carolina. He married his wife Sarah in June 2010. He has spoken to young adults across North America and has traveled to countries such as Botswana, South Africa, the Philippines, Greece, England, South Korea, France, Spain, Germany, Norway, and Brazil. Daniel loves music and reading dusty old literary classics.